Move Beyond 3

STUDENT'S BOOK

macmillan education

Robert Campbell
Rob Metcalf
Rebecca Robb Benne

STARTER

A DAY IN DYLAN'S LIFE

BEFORE SCHOOL

THINK AND READ

1 **Think of three activities you do before school. Compare with the class.**

2 **01 Read the story. Are your activities in the story?**

RECALL

1 **Write the words for Dylan's family members.**

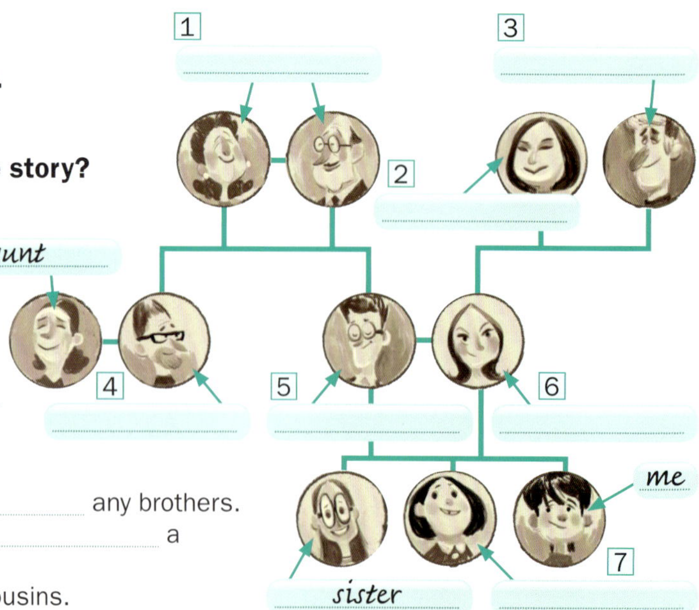

2 a **02 Complete the sentences about Dylan. Use *have* or *has*. Then listen and check.**

1 Dylan *has* a mom and a dad.
2 He ______ two sisters. He ______ any brothers.
3 Dylan's dad ______ a brother. He ______ a sister.
4 Dylan and his sisters ______ any cousins.
5 But they ______ four grandparents.

b **Work in pairs. Ask and answer questions about your family. Use the words in Exercise 1.**

Do you have a brother?

Yes, I do. His name is … / I have three brothers. / No, I don't.

3 a **Underline eight words for clothes in the story. Can you add four more words?**

b **What are your favorite clothes? Tell the class.**

4 ▶03 **Put the correct words together. Listen and check.**

In Dylan's bag there's a/an ...

1	note	key
2	lunch	case
3	class	book
4	text	box
5	pencil	schedule
6	house	book

5 a Complete the sentences. Use *there is/isn't* or *there are/aren't*.

In my sister's school bag ...

1 ✓ *there are* five notebooks.
2 ✓ .... a blue pencil case.
3 ✗ .... a class schedule.
4 ✓ .... a lunchbox.
5 ✗ .... a lot of textbooks.
6 ✗ .... a house key.

b Work in pairs. Ask and answer questions about what's in your school bag.

Is there a ... ?

Yes, there is. / No, there isn't.

Are there any ... ?

Yes, there are. / No, there aren't.

6 Work in pairs. Tell your partner about your morning routine.

I get up at six o'clock. I have breakfast at ...

AFTER SCHOOL

THINK AND READ

1 Check (✓) the things you usually do after school.

- cook ☐
- do homework ☐
- meet people ☐
- go swimming ☐
- read a book ☐

2 ▶04 Read the story. Which of the things in Exercise 1 does Dylan do today?

RECALL

1 ▶05 Put the words in order to make classroom phrases. Listen and check. Then listen again and repeat.

1 24. / your / Open / to / books / page
Open your books to page 24.
2 repeat / you / please? / Can / that,
....
3 the / don't / I / question. / understand
....
4 please? / the / go / I / bathroom, / Can / to
....
5 a / borrow / please? / I / Can / pen,
....
6 How / say / English? / you / do / in / "pizarra"
....

2 a ▶06 Which activities does Dylan like doing? Write sentences. Then listen and check.

1 ✓ cook *He likes cooking.*
2 ✓ listen to music ....
3 ✓ read ....
4 ✓ swim ....
5 ✗ act ....
6 ✗ speak Spanish ....

b Work in pairs. Tell a partner which activities in Exercise 2a you like and dislike. What other activities do you like?

I don't like reading.

I like playing basketball.

3 a 07 **Complete the conversation with the question words in the box. Then listen and check. Dylan doesn't like acting, but he says he loves drama. Why?**

How ~~What~~ When Where Who Why

Anna: (1) *What* time is it?
Dylan: It's 4:15. (2) ________ do you want to know?
Anna: I want to go to the drama club. (3) ________ does it start?
Dylan: At 4:30.
Anna: (4) ________ does the club meet? Do you know?
Dylan: In the auditorium.
Anna: (5) ________ long does it last?
Dylan: Forty-five minutes.
Anna: (6) ________ 's the teacher?
Dylan: Miss Harris. She's my class teacher.
Anna: Do you like drama?
Dylan: Um … yes, I love it.

b Work in pairs. Ask and answer questions about another school club in the story.

When does the cooking club start? *It starts at …*

4 a Read Dylan's homework and find the six false facts.

He doesn't have a brother.

b Write about your life and include three false facts. Show your description to a partner. Can your partner find the false facts?

My name's …

My name's Dylan. I'm 14 years old. I have two sisters and one brother. I always get up at 7:10. I have breakfast with my mom. School starts at 8:30. I wear jeans and sneakers to school. My teacher's name is Miss Green. I like her. I also like swimming and listening to music. I always tell the truth.

Workbook, pages 82–83

UNIT 1 SWITCH ON

IN THE PICTURE An app for everything

»» Talk about communication and technology

WORK WITH WORDS

1 RECALL **Work in pairs. Make a list of the devices you can see in the pictures. Can you add more things connected to communication and technology to your list? You have two minutes.**

2 **Match the icons (1–12) in the photo to the apps.**

mail	maps *1*	web browser .....
calendar	calculator	app store .....
games	notes	compass .....
videos	messages	social networking .....

3 08 **Listen and check your answers. Then listen and repeat.**

4 **a** 09 PRONOUNCE **Listen to the word. Underline the /æ/ sound.**

maps

b 10 **Listen and underline the /æ/ sound in the words. Then listen again and repeat the words.**

app store   calculator   calendar   camera   laptop   tablet

5 **Which app(s) can you use to …**

1 go on the internet? *web browser*
2 find north? .....
3 write to other people? .....
4 chat online with your friends? .....
5 do your math homework? .....
6 find your location or destination? .....
7 organize your time? .....
8 get new apps? .....

6 **Take the quiz.**

THE MINI APP QUIZ

HOW MUCH DO YOU KNOW ABOUT APPS?

TAKE THIS SHORT QUIZ TO FIND OUT!

		A	B	C
1	App is the abbreviation for …	application.	apple.	appliance.
2	An app is …	an icon.	a device.	a program.
3	The first online app store opened in …	1999.	2003.	2008.

SPEAK

7 Work in pairs. Do one of the tasks.

1 Decide which three apps in Exercise 2 are the most useful. Explain why.

2 Invent a new app. What's it called? What can it do? Tell other students about it.

PHRASE BYTES

I think … are the most useful because …

Our new app's called … and it can …

8 THE MOVING PICTURE Watch four teenagers talking about apps. Which ones do they use? What are their favorite apps?

MOVE BEYOND

Do the Words & Beyond exercise on page 69.

Workbook, page 84

»» Understand new words

SPEAK AND READ

1 Work in pairs. Read the sentences. Are they true for you? If not, explain why.

1 I have a lot of free time.
2 I listen to music or watch TV when I do my homework.
3 It's hard for me to relax at home.

2 (11) Read the first paragraph of the magazine article. Underline the words you don't know.

3 a Read the tips in the HOW TO box.

b Write definitions for the words you underlined in Exercise 2. Use the tips in the HOW TO box to help you. Don't use a dictionary.

4 Work in pairs. Exchange your definitions. Can your partner find the correct words in the text?

HOW TO
understand new words

- Identify the type of word (verb, noun, adjective, adverb).
- Compare it to your language. Is there a similar word? Does its meaning help you?
- Look at the words and sentences before and after the new word.

Do you need to switch off more?

How often do you do nothing? For a lot of young people, the answer is never. When we sit down and relax, we're always doing something. We watch TV, listen to music, or send text messages. We sometimes do all three at the same time. We hardly ever just sit quietly and stop thinking. Our brain uses a lot of energy during the day and gets tired. We need to stop thinking and switch off from time to time. Switching off helps us to relax completely and feel full of energy again.

Do you need to switch off more? Answer the questions in the survey to find out.

How often do you do these things? Mark your answers.

A = once a day or more
B = often, but not every day
C = sometimes
D = rarely or never

	A	B	C	D
1 Watch TV	○	○	○	○
2 Listen to music	○	○	○	○
3 Play video games	○	○	○	○
4 Call friends	○	○	○	○
5 Send text messages	○	○	○	○
6 Read and send emails	○	○	○	○
7 Use a social networking site	○	○	○	○
8 Chat online with friends	○	○	○	○
9 Go on the internet	○	○	○	○
10 Watch videos on the internet	○	○	○	○

Calculate your score (A = 3; B = 2; C = 1; D = 0).
Then read the explanation for your score.

Scores and explanations

0–10	You regularly do nothing. Don't stop switching off!
11–20	You do nothing once or twice a week, but it's good to switch off more often.
21–30	You rarely switch off. Find 10 minutes a day to do nothing.

5 Take the survey in the magazine article and calculate your score. Then read the explanation for your score.

PHRASE BYTES
I agree / don't agree with it. I often / never …
It's hard because …
Of course it's possible! / It's impossible because …

REACT

6 Work in pairs. What do you think? Tell your partner.

1 Do you agree with the explanation? Why or why not?
2 Why is it hard to switch off?
3 Is it possible to do your homework well if you listen to music at the same time?

MOVE BEYOND
Put the 10 activities in the survey in order, with your favorite activity first. Then compare your list with a partner. Talk about what's similar and what's different.

Workbook, page 85

GRAMMAR Simple present, adverbs, and expressions of frequency

Talk about how often you do things

READ Grammar in context

1 Read the conversation. Why isn't Dan happy?

Dan: Do you use the class blog?
Carla: Yes, I do. But I only log on **from time to time**. How often do you use it?
Dan: I log on after school **every day**. I **always** log on on weekends too.
Carla: I **rarely** log on during the week. I don't have time. I **occasionally** log on on the weekend, but my brother uses the computer a lot.
Dan: Oh, OK. So that's why you don't see my messages.

STUDY

2 Choose the correct option.

Simple present

Use the simple present for habits, routines, and things that are generally true.

Affirmative and negative forms
With *I, you, we, they,* don't add the letter s to the end of the verb. With *he, she, it,* add the letter s.
I log on after school every day.
My brother uses the computer a lot.
With *I, you, we, they,* use ***don't* / *doesn't*** + verb.
I don't have time.
With *he, she, it,* use ***don't* / *doesn't*** + verb.
He doesn't let me use the computer.

Questions and short answers
Use *do* with *I, you, we, they*. Use *does* with *he, she, it*.
***Do* / *Does* you use the class blog? Yes, I *do* / *does*.**

See GRAMMAR DATABASE, page 64.

3 Choose the correct option.

Adverbs and expressions of frequency

Use adverbs and expressions of frequency to say how often you do things.

Word order
Put adverbs ***before* / *after*** action verbs.
Put adverbs ***before* / *after*** the verb *to be*.
I occasionally log on on weekends.
My brother is always busy on the computer.
Put expressions of frequency at the beginning or the ***middle* / *end*** of a sentence.
I log on every day.

Use this chart to remember adverb frequencies.

0% never
hardly ever, rarely
sometimes, occasionally
often, regularly
usually, normally
100% always

See GRAMMAR DATABASE, page 64.

PRACTICE

4 Complete the interview with the simple present form of the verbs.

Sonia: Excuse me. I'm doing a survey about cell phones. (1) *Does your cell phone have* (your cell phone / have) a camera?
Jude: Yes, it (2) ______ (do).
Sonia: How often (3) ______ (you / use) it?
Jude: Hardly ever. The photos (4) ______ (look) terrible.
Sonia: So you (5) ______ (not take) photos with your cell phone.
Jude: I always (6) ______ (use) my dad's camera. It takes great pictures.

5 a Put the adverbs and expressions in the correct place in the sentences.

1 I check my email. (often)
I often check my email.
2 I can't play video games. (every day)
______
3 I listen to music when I do my homework. (occasionally)
______
4 I watch videos on the internet. (from time to time)
______
5 My cell phone is turned on. (rarely)
______
6 I send text messages to friends. (now and then)
______

b Change the false sentences to make them true for you.

6 Prepare a survey. Write questions with *How often* about these ways to contact your friends.

call chat online send emails send text messages

How often ...

SPEAK

7 Work in pairs. Ask the questions in your survey and note the answers. Then tell another pair the results of your survey.

Paul sends emails ...

Workbook, pages 86–87

LISTENING AND VOCABULARY Raspberry Pi

»» Listen for the main ideas

WORK WITH WORDS

1 Work in pairs. Answer the questions.

1 How often do you study computers at school?
2 Do you like studying computers? Why or why not?

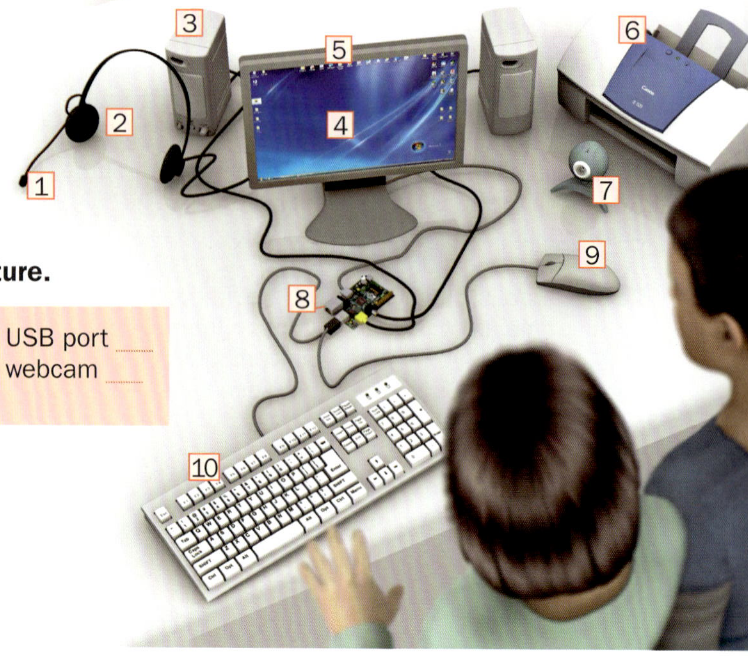

2 Match the computer parts to things in the picture.

headphones ___	monitor ___	screen ___	USB port ___
keyboard ___	mouse ___	speaker ___	webcam ___
microphone ___	printer ___		

3 ▶12 Listen and check your answers. Then listen and repeat.

4 Which thing(s) do you use …

1 to write with? *keyboard*
2 to listen to things? ______ ______
3 to see things? ______ ______ ______
4 to connect things? ______

LISTEN

5 a Read the tips in the HOW TO box.

b ▶13 Listen to the news report from a school website. Choose the best summary of the report.

1 A school has a lot of new computers for its computer classes.
2 A class is learning how to create computer games.
3 A school is using a small computer to teach students how computers work.

HOW TO

listen for the main ideas

- [ ] Don't worry if you can't understand everything.
- [ ] Listen for words you already know.
- [ ] Use these words to help you understand important ideas.

6 Which tips in the HOW TO box did you use for help with Exercise 5b? Check (✓) them.

7 ▶13 Listen again and choose the correct answer.

1 Tom Smith is …
A a teacher. B at his school. C at a different school.
2 The Raspberry Pi is …
A cheap. B simple. C a French invention.
3 Students use the Raspberry Pi to …
A learn to write code. B watch TV. C play games on the internet.
4 The report ends because …
A the Pi stops working. B it's lunchtime. C Tom has no more questions.

REACT

8 Work in pairs. What do you think? Tell your partner.

1 Do you have a computer? What do you use it for?
2 Do you think it's important for students to learn to write code? Why or why not?

MOVE BEYOND

Do the Words & Beyond exercise on page 69.

PHRASE BYTES

I use my / our computer at home to …
I think / don't think it's important because …

Workbook, pages 88–89

GRAMMAR Articles: *a/an*, *the*, and zero article

Use *a/an*, *the*, and zero article to refer to things

READ Grammar in context

1 Read the description. What's unusual about the school? Why?

We're at (1) a school in (2) Silicon Valley in (3) the United States, the location of many of (4) the biggest technology companies in (5) the world. It's called The Waldorf School of the Peninsula, and many Silicon Valley workers send their children here. When you go into (6) the school, you get a surprise. There is no technology, just (7) books and blackboards. Why? As (8) the teachers say, a computer is not (9) a teacher!

STUDY

2 Match the underlined examples in Exercise 1 to the explanations.

Articles: *a/an*, *the*, and zero article

Articles indicate if something is a general or specific example.

a/an +	one example of a thing 1 a job ___
the +	a specific thing ___ the only example of a thing 5 superlatives and dates ___ something mentioned before 6 plural place names ___
zero article +	things in general ___ meals, days, singular place names 2

See GRAMMAR DATABASE, page 64.

PRACTICE

3 Complete the sentences. Write *the* if necessary. If not, write (–).

1 At my school there are – computers in every classroom.
2 ___ computer room has a computer for every student.
3 One day ___ schools will stop using ___ textbooks.
4 ___ internet is ___ best way to learn ___ things about ___ world.

4 Choose the correct options to complete the conversation.

Paul: I need to check my email. Do you have (1) (a) / *the* / – computer?
Ray: Yes, I do. It's in (2) *a* / *the* / – kitchen.
Paul: That's (3) *a* / *the* / – strange place to keep it!
Ray: It's (4) *a* / *the* / – laptop, and I always do my homework there. It's (5) *a* / *the* / – quietest place in (6) *a* / *the* / – house!

5 Complete Ellen's description with *a, an, the,* or zero article (–).

I study at a middle school in (1) a suburb of (2) ___ Sydney in (3) ___ Australia called (4) ___ Ashfield. For me, (5) ___ best lesson of the week is computers. We have (6) ___ really good teacher, and I love learning how (7) ___ computers work. It's (8) ___ last lesson before (9) ___ lunch on (10) ___ Tuesday. (11) ___ teacher also organizes (12) ___ extra class at lunchtime on Mondays and I always go to it. I'm not very good at other subjects, but I always get good grades in computer class.

SPEAK

6 Work in pairs. Take turns choosing a topic. Can you speak for 30 seconds about the topic without stopping?

- computers
- the USA
- my school
- Sunday
- the internet
- English
- breakfast
- my birthday

Workbook, page 90

LANGUAGE & BEYOND

GET ORGANIZED

»» Use lists to help you organize your time

THURSDAY

FRIDAY

SATURDAY

READ

1 **Work in pairs. Look at Jasmin's bulletin board above. Copy and complete her planner for Thursday, Friday, and Saturday.**

2 **Look at the planner. Is it easy for Jasmin to do everything? Why or why not?**

DO

3 **Work in pairs. Help Jasmin organize her time.**

1 Decide which activities on each day are more important than others.
2 Decide which activities she possibly doesn't have time to do.
3 Find a time for her to buy a present.

PHRASE BYTES

I think … is / are more important than … because …

I agree / don't agree.

I don't think she has time to …

She can … if she has time.

On Saturday maybe she can … first and then …

REFLECT

4 **Discuss the questions with your class. Do you agree with the REFLECTION POINT?**

1 Was it easy or hard to organize Jasmin's time? Why?
2 Will it be easy or hard for you to organize your time this week? Why?
3 How do you feel when your time isn't organized?

REFLECTION POINT

It's a good idea to make a list of things you need to do during the week, and then decide which ones are more important than others. Making a list helps you organize your time and not get stressed.

EXTEND

5 **Make a list of the things you need to do over the next three days. Then put the things in order, with the most important ones first.**

6 **Work in groups. Show other students your list and explain how you decided on the best order to do things.**

»» Workbook, page 93

SPEAKING Say what you think

Ask for and give opinions

SPEAK

1 Work in pairs. Answer the questions.

1 Do you watch videos like these on the internet? Why or why not?
2 What do you think happens next in each video?

LISTEN

2 ▶14 Listen to the conversation. What do the friends think about the video?

Adam: Hey, guys. Watch this! … So, what do you (1) ____________ about it?
Laura: I (2) ____________ it's OK. I don't (3) ____________ it's very original, but it's funny.
Adam: What do you (4) ____________ , Tina?
Tina: I don't (5) ____________ . I (6) ____________ it's kind of funny, but it's also a little mean.
Adam: Mean?
Tina: Yes. Do you (7) ____________ the dog's happy?
Adam: No, maybe not.
Ben: Hey, what are you doing with my tablet?
Laura: We're watching that video.
Ben: So what do you (8) ____________ about it? Just funny, or really, really funny?

3 ▶14 Complete the conversation with *think* or *know*. Then listen again to check.

4 Make this opinion negative. Use the conversation to help you.
I think it's very original.

5 ▶15 Listen and repeat the expressions from the conversation.

ACT

6 Work in groups of three or four. Ask for and give your opinions about these things. Give reasons.

cell phone ads   computer classes   computers
social networking sites   the internet   video games

PHRASEBOOK ▶16

Ask for opinions
What do you think about … ?
What do you think?
Do you think … ?

Give opinions
I think it's funny / boring / expensive.
I think they're funny / boring / expensive.
I don't think …
I don't know.

Workbook, page 91

WRITING Could you live without your cell phone?

»» Use the correct word order

READ

1 **Read the answers to the website question. Which one is closer to your answer? Why?**

open views gadget news &views

home news reviews forum

The tech zone question

Could you live without your cell phone? Here are some of your answers!

Yes ✓

I could easily live without it. I have a really old phone, and I don't need another one. I hardly ever use it. People sometimes call me, but I prefer to talk to friends face to face. Other people in my class play with their cell phones all the time and never actually talk to their friends when they meet!

No ✗

I couldn't live without my cell phone. It's the most important thing I own. I do everything with it. I use it every day to update my profile, go on the web, check mail, organize my time, and play games. I rarely call friends because I never have time, but I send text messages about 20 times a day.

2 **a** **Read the tips in the HOW TO box.**

b **Find two examples of each tip in the website answers.**

HOW TO

use the correct word order

- Start sentences with subject + verb + object (SVO).
- Put adverbs of frequency before the main verb.
- Put expressions of frequency after SVO.
- Put adjectives, including comparatives / superlatives, before nouns.

PRACTICE

3 **Put the words in order to make sentences. Use the HOW TO box to help you.**

1 games / all day. / I / on my phone / play
I play games on my phone all day.

2 send / rarely / text messages. / I

3 every / my / I / call / friends / night. / best

4 I'm / right now. / for browsing the web / app / using / new / a

5 hardly / videos / watch / I / on my cell phone. / ever

DISCUSS

4 **Give reasons to have or not to have a cell phone.**

WRITE

5 **Write five reasons to have or not to have a cell phone. Use complete sentences.**

1 Put the most important reasons first. End with reasons that are funny or not very important.

2 Use correct word order. Normal word order is: subject + verb + object. See the HOW TO box.

3 Use adverbs of frequency and time expressions to describe how often you use your cell phone.

SHARE

6 **Debate your answers with other students. What are some other devices you can or can't live without?**

»» Workbook, pages 92–93

VOCABULARY Applications (Apps)

1 Complete the names of the apps.

The Computer Museum | **The first apps**

1 g _ _ _ s
2 m _ _ s
3 n _ _ _ s
4 me _ _ _ _ _ s
5 m _ _ _
6 v _ _ _ _ s
7 cal _ _ _ _ _
8 cal _ _ _ _ _ _ _
9 so _ _ _ _ net _ _ _ _ _ _ _
10 app s _ _ _ _

___ /10

Computer parts

2 The names of the computer parts are all wrong. Write the correct names.

1 ______ 5 ______
2 ______ 6 ______
3 ______ 7 ______
4 ______ 8 ______

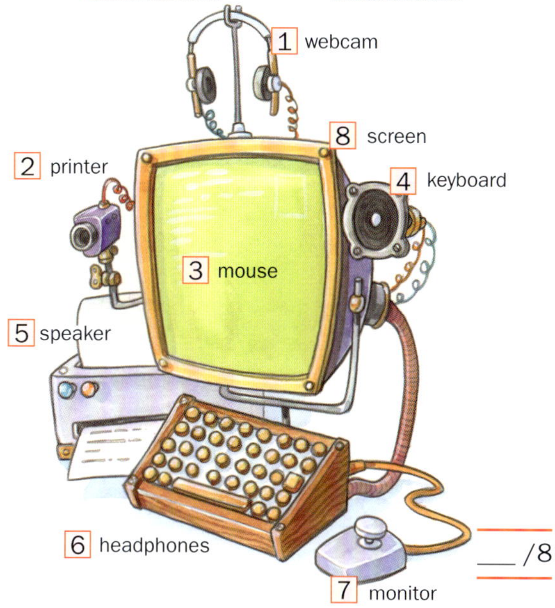

___ /8

GRAMMAR Simple present, adverbs, and expressions of frequency

3 Choose the correct options to complete the conversation.

A: The Computer Museum. How can I help you?
B: Hello. (1) ***You*** / ***Do you*** open at lunchtime?
A: Yes, (2) ***we're always*** / ***we always are*** open at lunchtime.
B: How much (3) ***do*** / ***does*** tickets cost?
A: It's free for children and adults (4) ***pay*** / ***pays*** $5.
B: Is there a restaurant? We'd like to have lunch there.
A: The museum (5) ***doesn't*** / ***don't*** have a restaurant, but the café (6) ***normally has*** / ***has normally*** some sandwiches.
B: Normally?
A: Well, (7) ***from time to time we get*** / ***we from time to time get*** a lot of visitors in the morning, and we (8) ***run*** / ***runs*** out of sandwiches.

___ /16

Articles: *a/an*, *the*, and zero article

4 Complete the description with *a/an*, *the*, or zero article (–).

WeAreFriends was one of (1) ______ first internet websites. It was (2) ______ social networking site for (3) ______ teenagers, and when it closed in 1996 it had over 3,000 users around (4) ______ world. The creator of (5) ______ website, (6) ______ student named Steve Watzupi, ran WeAreFriends from (7) ______ small Amstrong computer, and the site closed when his computer stopped working. His house in (8) ______ Oxford is now a museum.

___ /16

Your score: ___ /50

SKILLS CHECK

✓✓✓ Yes, I can. No problem!
✓✓ Yes, I can. But I need a little help.
✓ Yes, I can. But I need a lot of help.

I can understand new words when I read. ______
I can listen for the main ideas. ______
I can use lists to help me organize my time. ______
I can ask for and give opinions. ______
I can use the correct word order when I write. ______

Workbook, pages 94–95

UNIT

2 HOME AND AWAY

IN THE PICTURE Three apartments

Talk about homes and household chores

WORK WITH WORDS

1 RECALL **Work in pairs. Make lists of words under the headings. Use the picture to help you. You have three minutes.**

Kinds of homes	Rooms	Furniture	Appliances	Other
apartment	*kitchen*	*bed*	*refrigerator*	*clock*

2 17 **Write the names of the people in the boxes in the picture. Then listen and check.**

1 Ethan is making his bed.
2 Linda is loading the dishwasher.
3 Alyssa is setting the table.
4 Nick is vacuuming his room.
5 Tyler is doing the laundry.
6 Josh is mopping the floor.

3 18 **What are the people doing one hour later? Listen and write.**

~~clear the table~~ do the ironing sort the recycling
take out the trash vacuum wash the dishes

1 Josh is *clearing the table* .
2 Alyssa is ………………………… .
3 Nick is ………………………… .
4 Ethan is ………………………… .
5 Tyler is ………………………… .
6 Linda is ………………………… .

4 19 **Listen and check. Then listen and repeat.**

5 THE MOVING PICTURE **Watch the video. What is Tyler doing?**

6 **Work in pairs. Mime one of the chores in Exercise 2 or 3. Can your partner say what you are doing?**

Are you setting the table? *Yes, I am. / No, I'm not.*

7 a 20 PRONOUNCE **Listen to the word. Underline the silent letter.**

make

b 21 **Listen and underline the silent letters in the words. Then listen again and repeat the words.**

hour island knife listen load Wednesday

SPEAK

8 Work in pairs. Answer the questions.

1 How often do you make your bed?
never / *rarely* / *sometimes* / *often* / *always*

2 How often do you clean your room?
never / *rarely* / *sometimes* / *often* / *always*

3 Who usually does these chores in your home?
do the laundry / *do the ironing* / *mop the floor* / *set the table* / *take out the trash* / *vacuum* / *wash the dishes*

MOVE BEYOND

Do the Words & Beyond exercise on page 70.

READING Living together

Understand the main ideas

SPEAK AND READ

1 Work in pairs. Answer the questions.

1 What type of building do you live in?
2 How many people live in your home? Who are they?

2 a Read the tips in the HOW TO box.

b 22 Read the article quickly and choose the best description.

A A description of life in three New York apartments.
B A teenage boy's view of life with his family.
C An official report on teenagers in New York.

HOW TO

understand the main ideas

- [ ] Read the text quickly.
- [ ] Don't try to understand every word.
- [ ] Think about the general topic.
- [ ] Look for important and repeated words and sentences.

It's 6:15 p.m. in New York City. In a third-floor apartment on Broome Street, Liyu Wang is cooking dinner for his family. His wife, Victoria, is setting the table, and their two sons – Ethan, age 15, and Nicholas, age 14 – are cleaning their room. The boys' sister – Alexis, age 11 – is in the living room, doing her homework. Her grandfather is sitting on the sofa watching television, while Felix the cat is watching the family's pet fish.

In New York, it's common for several generations of a family to live in the same home. One in ten households has three generations or more. As Ethan explains, living together has its advantages and disadvantages.

"We have a lot of relatives in New York, and our home is like a meeting place for everyone. Every day we see our cousins, uncles, aunts … It's a fun place," he says. But communication can be difficult. "My dad is originally from China, and my grandpa doesn't speak much English. And we're just kids, you know. We see life in a different way. So sometimes we argue. But I think that's normal."

Ethan doesn't only argue with his father and grandfather. "There isn't a lot of space here, and I share a bedroom with my brother, Nick. So sometimes it's hard, you know, to be alone … to study. And Nick never cleans the room. Mom says, 'How can you live in this mess?' Mom and I argue a lot. I forget to do things like feeding the fish or sorting the recycling."

3 Check (✓) the information in the article.

Description of a family.	✓	Interview with a parent.	
Facts about families in New York.		The opinions of a teenage family member.	
Information about family life in China.			

4 Which tips in the HOW TO box did you use for help with Exercises 2b and 3? Check (✓) them.

5 Read the article again to decide if each statement is correct (*C*) or incorrect (*I*).

1 The Wang family is similar to a lot of other families in New York. *C*
2 The rest of the family lives in China. ____
3 Ethan doesn't like family life. ____
4 The apartment is very large. ____
5 Nicholas doesn't help clean the bedroom. ____
6 Ethan rarely argues with his mother. ____

REACT

6 Work in pairs. What do you think? Tell your partner.

1 Is the Wang home similar to your home? In what ways is it similar or different?
2 Do you often argue with people at home?

MOVE BEYOND

Look at the picture on pages 18–19 and describe what is happening in one of the other apartments.

Workbook, page 97

GRAMMAR Present progressive and simple present

Talk about things happening now, and about habits and routines

READ AND LISTEN Grammar in context

1 (23) **Read and listen to the phone conversation. Why is Beth calling Jake?**

Beth: Hi, Jake? It's Beth. What are you doing now?
Jake: Oh, hi, Beth. I'm at the pool. Right now I'm waiting for swim practice to start. I always swim on Thursdays, remember?
Beth: Well, I'm studying for the math test, and I need help.
Jake: What's wrong?
Beth: I don't understand some of the calculations.
Jake: Are you studying at the library?
Beth: Yes.
Jake: Pete studies at the library on Thursdays. Ask him for help.
Beth: Thanks!

STUDY

2 Complete the explanations with the correct tense.

Present progressive and simple present

Use the ______ for habits, routines, and things that are generally true.
Pete studies at the library on Thursdays.

Use the ______ with adverbs of frequency.
I always swim on Thursdays.

Use the ______ with stative verbs that describe thinking or feeling, such as *like, know, need*, or *understand.*
I don't understand some of the calculations.

Use the ______ for actions in progress now or with time expressions such as *right now* or *today*.
Right now I'm waiting for swim practice to start.

See GRAMMAR DATABASE, page 65.

PRACTICE

3 Complete the conversation with the present progressive form of the verbs.

Rob: Hello, Jake. What (1) *are you doing* (you / do) here?
Jake: I (2) ______ (look) for Carlos. Is he here?
Rob: No. I think he (3) ______ (play) soccer with the others.
Jake: No. They (4) ______ (not / practice) this morning.
Rob: Maybe he (5) ______ (shop) with Nestor in town.
Jake: I don't think so. He (6) ______ (study) for a test.

4 Choose the correct options.

It's 6 a.m. Adam and Shannon (1) *wake up* / (*are waking up*) their brothers and sisters. It's not a quick job – there are 11 of them!

With 13 kids in the house, the family (2) *needs* / *is needing* good organization. The kids (3) *usually take* / *are usually taking* turns doing the chores.

It's now 7 a.m., and Mia (4) *wash* / *is washing* the dishes. At the same time, Adam and Shannon (5) *vacuum* / *are vacuuming* and (6) *clean* / *cleaning* the house.

The kids (7) *spend* / *are spending* weekdays at school and (8) *come* / *are coming* home at 4 p.m.

On Fridays the family (9) *always has* / *is always having* a pizza night. It's now 7 p.m. and everyone (10) *eats* / *is eating* pizza together in the kitchen.

5 Check (✓) the correct option in the conversation. Then underline the stative verbs.

1 a "Mom? Are you liking doing the laundry?"
  b "Mom? Do you like doing the laundry?" ✓
2 a "I don't understand the question."
  b "I'm not understanding the question."
3 a "I'm needing a clean shirt to go to the movies."
  b "I need a clean shirt to go to the movies."
4 a "There's a clean shirt in the basket. You know how to iron."
  b "There's a clean shirt in the basket. You're knowing how to iron."
5 a "I'm hating ironing."
  b "I hate ironing."

SPEAK

6 Work in pairs. Say a day and a time to your partner. Can your partner describe what he or she is doing or normally does?

It's seven o'clock in the morning on Tuesday. What are you doing?

I'm having breakfast and getting ready for school.

Do you always have breakfast at seven o'clock?

I normally have breakfast at 7:00 on school days. On the weekend I have breakfast at 9:00.

LISTENING AND VOCABULARY Soap opera

Understand a situation

SPEAK AND LISTEN

1 Work in pairs. Answer the questions.

1 A soap opera is a television series about the imaginary lives of a group of people. Which soap operas are popular in your country?
2 Do you watch any soap operas? If so, which ones? If not, why not?
3 Choose a soap opera or a TV drama. Where does the story take place? Who are the people in the story?

2 a Read the tips in the HOW TO box.

b 24 Listen to an excerpt from a soap opera and answer the questions.

1 Who are the people?
2 Where are they?
3 What are they talking about?

KEIRA: Hiya, Sal.
SAL: Hi!
JACK: What's up? You don't look very happy.
SAL: Nothing.

3 Which tips in the HOW TO box did you use for help with Exercise 2b? Check (✓) them.

4 24 Listen again and match the sentence halves.

1 Jack ...	is leaving the group.
2 Keira ...	isn't speaking to Sal.
3 Mr. Gibbons ...	is playing in two weeks.
4 Tom ...	is going ice skating on Saturday morning.
5 Sal ...	is hanging out with Lizzie and Sharon in the afternoon.
6 The group ...	has some good news.

HOW TO
understand a situation

☐ Listen for important and repeated words.
☐ Listen to how people talk. Do they know each other?
☐ Listen for names and sounds.

REACT

5 Work in pairs. What do you think? Tell your partner.

1 What do Keira, Tom, and Jack say to Mr. Gibbons next?
2 What happens at the concert?

WORK WITH WORDS

6 a Match the free-time activities to the pictures.

____ **go** ice skating
____ **do** judo
____ **play** an instrument
____ **go** to acting class
____ **collect** cards
____ **use** social networking sites
____ **visit** exhibitions
____ **read** magazines
____ **hang out** with friends
____ **watch** online videos

b Add more free-time activities using the verbs in Exercise 6a.

7 Work in pairs. Talk about your weekend free-time activities.

On Saturdays, I usually do judo.

I always go ice skating on Saturday morning.

MOVE BEYOND
Do the Words & Beyond exercise on page 70.

Workbook, pages 100–101

READ AND LISTEN »» Grammar in context

1 ▶25 **Read and listen to the conversation. What are Mario and Fiona doing on the weekend?**

Mario: What are you doing on the weekend? The soccer team's playing on Saturday.
Fiona: Where are you playing? Is it a home game?
Mario: No. We're playing away in Newton. Can you come?
Fiona: I can't. I'm helping Dad clean the house this weekend. My cousin is coming to stay next week.
Mario: How long is he staying?
Fiona: *He's* actually a *she*. And she's leaving at the end of the month.

STUDY

2 Complete the explanation. Use Exercise 1 to help you.

Present progressive for future arrangements

Use the present progressive for events or plans that will happen in the future.
The football team ________ *on Saturday.*

Use a time expression to indicate the future.
What are you doing ________*?*

See GRAMMAR DATABASE, page 65.

PRACTICE

3 Write the questions about the conversation in Exercise 1.

1 What / day / Mario / play / on the weekend?
What day is Mario playing on the weekend?
2 Where / the team / play?
____
3 Who / Fiona / help / on Saturday?
____
4 Why / they / clean / the house?
____
5 When / Fiona's cousin / leave?
____

4 Answer the questions in Exercise 3.

5 Write sentences about Mario's plans for next week.

On Monday he's going ice skating at 5:30 p.m.

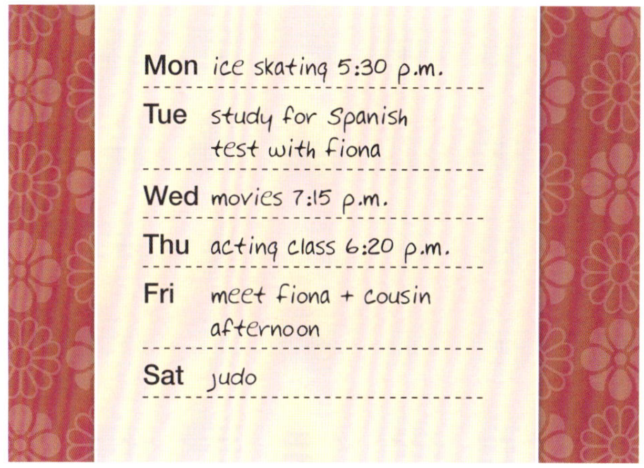

6 Order the time expressions starting with the most recent.

____ this weekend
____ next year
____ at 7 p.m.
____ this afternoon
____ next week
____ tomorrow
1 right now
____ tonight
____ in two weeks

7 Complete the sentences with your arrangements.

1 This evening ________
2 On the weekend ________
3 Next month ________
4 In the summer ________

SPEAK

8 Work in pairs. Complete the tasks.

1 Student A looks at the plans on page 75. Student B looks at the plans on page 76.
2 Ask and answer questions about the days. Find a time to go to the movies together.

What are you doing on Friday afternoon?

I'm having a guitar lesson and then I'm going to Sal's party. What about you?

I'm going to the Science Museum. I'm free on Saturday morning.

I'm not free. I'm going shopping with Tom.

LANGUAGE & BEYOND

Identify the cause of a problem

GET THINKING

SPEAK AND READ

1 **Work in pairs. Look at the pictures above. What's the problem?**

2 **Work in pairs. Student A reads Lauren's point of view and Student B reads Grace's point of view.**

3 **Explain the point of view you read to your partner.**

Lauren's unhappy because ... *Grace says that ...*

Lauren's point of view

Grace always starts watching TV while I'm trying to do my homework. I know she's my older sister, but I can't concentrate when the TV's on. It's not fair.

Grace's point of view

Mom and Dad give me all the household chores to do. While I'm mopping the floors, Lauren's pretending to do her homework and laughing at me. It's not fair.

DO

4 **Work in groups. Answer the questions.**

1 Which of the sisters has a problem – Grace, Lauren, or both?
2 Do they understand each other's problem(s)?
3 In what way are the problems similar?

5 **Work in groups. Think of solutions to the problems.**

They can take turns ... *Lauren/Grace can ...*

REFLECT

6 **Discuss the questions with your class. Do you agree with the REFLECTION POINT?**

1 Share your suggestions from Exercise 5 with the rest of the class. Which suggestions are most helpful and why?
2 Do you know people in a similar situation? What are their problems?
3 Do you find it easy to talk about problems you have with other people?

REFLECTION POINT

Sometimes we don't understand a problem because we only see one point of view. When you can see the different points of view, it's easier to find a solution.

EXTEND

7 **Work in groups. Read about Ethan's problems. Think of ways he can find a solution to his problems.**

"There isn't a lot of space here, and I share a bedroom with my brother, Nick. So sometimes it's hard to be alone ... to study. And Nick never cleans the room. Mom says, 'How can you live in this mess?' We argue a lot. I forget to do things like feeding the fish or sorting the recycling."

Workbook, page 105

SPEAKING On the phone

Check that you understand on the phone

SPEAK

1 Work in pairs. Answer the questions.

1 Do you have a phone at home?
2 If so, what type of phone is it – a landline, a cell phone, or an internet phone?
3 How often do people call the phone?

LISTEN

2 ▶26 Listen to the conversation. Who does Matt want to speak to and why?

Kate: Hello?
Matt: (1) ______
Kate: Hi, Matt. Keith isn't here right now.
Matt: (2) ______
Kate: Yes. Hold on. Let me get a pen … OK. I'm ready.
Matt: (3) ______
Kate: Sorry? Can you say that again? It's a bad connection.
Matt: (4) ______
Kate: How do you spell that?
Matt: (5) ______
Kate: Outside the Treetop coffee shop. At eight o'clock … Sorry. You're breaking up. I can't hear you. Could you repeat that?
Matt: (6) ______
Kate: 555-348-7792. OK.
Matt: (7) ______
Kate: Bye.

3 a Read the tips in the HOW TO box.

b ▶27 Complete the phrases from the conversation. Listen and check. Then listen and repeat.

1 Sorry? Can you *say that again* ?
2 It's a ______ .
3 How do you ______ ?
4 Sorry. You're ______ .
5 I can't ______ .
6 Could you ______ ?

4 What does Matt say? Complete the conversation in Exercise 2 with the sentences.

a Can I leave a message?
b T-r-e-e-t-o-p.
c Hi. It's Matt. Can I speak to Keith?
d If there's a problem, he can call me at 555-348-7792.
e Thanks, Kate. Bye.
f I'm calling from the train. I said we're all meeting at 8:00 outside the Treetop coffee shop.
g Tell him we're …

5 ▶28 Listen to the complete conversation. Then read it out loud with a partner.

6 Write Kate's note for Keith.

ACT

7 In groups of four, complete the tasks.

1 In pairs, prepare a message to leave in a phone conversation.
2 Take turns calling a student in the other pair. Ask to speak to someone who isn't there and leave a message.
3 Can the other student write the correct message?

HOW TO

check that you understand on the phone

- Be polite.
- Explain the problem.
- Ask the other person to repeat if you're not sure.

PHRASEBOOK ▶29

Phone phrases

Hello. It's … Can I speak to … ?
I'm calling from …
Hold on.
Can I leave a message? / Do you want to leave a message?
She / He can call me at …

Check that you understand

Could you repeat that?
Can you say that again?
How do you spell that?

Workbook, page 103

WRITING My status update

››› Use *and*, *also*, and *too*

SPEAK AND READ

1 **Work in pairs. Look at the photos of San Antonio and describe them.**

PHRASE BYTES

This is a photo of …

I think this is …

2 **Read the status updates. Which of the places isn't mentioned in the updates?**

a

b

c

d

e

1

Four hours ago

It's Sunday, our last day here. We're going to an aquarium to see whales. We're also having pizza tonight. San Antonio's a fantastic place.

Like · Comment · Share

2

Yesterday at 11:42 a.m.

It's day two of our weekend in San Antonio and we're sitting in a boat on the river. Dad is taking me up the Tower of the Americas this afternoon.

Like · Comment · Share

3

Friday at 7:18 p.m.

I'm away with my family in San Antonio. We're staying in a big hotel near downtown. San Antonio has a lot of restaurants and shops. Click here to see some photos. You can watch a video too.

Like · Comment · Share

3 **a** **Read the tips in the HOW TO box.**

b **Find examples of *and*, *too*, and *also* in the status updates in Exercise 2.**

HOW TO

use *and*, *also*, and *too*

- Use *and* to link two parts of a sentence.
- Use *also* and *too* to add another fact.
- Use *too* at the end of a sentence.
- Use *also* **after** *be* and *can*, and **before** other verbs.

PRACTICE

4 **Write the sentences with the words in parentheses.**

1 I'm listening to music. I'm reading a magazine. (also)
I'm listening to music. I'm also reading a magazine.

2 I like traveling. I like staying at home. (too)

3 It's raining. The bus is late. (and)

4 I love reading. Ana loves books. (also)

5 This evening I'm meeting friends. We're going to the movies. (and)

6 New York is an amazing city. San Antonio is an interesting place. (too)

DISCUSS

5 **Plan a dream vacation and talk about the fun activities you would like to do.**

WRITE

6 **Write a status update about your dream vacation.**

1 Describe where you are, what you're doing, how you feel, and what you're doing later in the day.

2 Use the present progressive to describe activities happening now and in the near future.

3 Use *too*, *and*, and *also* to connect your ideas. See the HOW TO box.

SHARE

7 **Take turns describing your dream vacation. Which vacation would you like to take? Which vacation would you not like to take?**

Workbook, pages 104–105

VOCABULARY Homes and household chores

1 Write the missing words.

Meet Harry, your new household helper. Harry does all those terrible household chores. He can (1) m ______ your bed in the morning and (2) c ______ the rooms. He can (3) v ______ and (4) m ______ the floors. When you need clean clothes, he can do the (5) l ______ and the (6) i ______ . He can (7) s ______ and (8) c ______ the table, and (9) w ______ the dishes or load the (10) d ______ . Before you go to bed, he can sort the (11) r ______ and take out the (12) t ______ . Put a Harry in your life and have more free time.

___ /12

Free-time activities

2 Complete the free-time activities you can do while Harry is cleaning. Use the verbs in the box.

collect do go hang out go play read use visit watch

1 ______ exhibitions
2 ______ to acting class
3 ______ judo
4 ______ an instrument
5 ______ magazines
6 ______ ice skating
7 ______ with friends
8 ______ social networking sites
9 ______ online videos
10 ______ cards

___ /10

GRAMMAR Present progressive and simple present

3 Complete the postcard with the simple present or present progressive form of the verbs.

Hi, Harry!

How are you? (1) ______ (I / write) *this postcard in Barcelona. The* (2) ______ (sun / shine) *and* (3) ______ (I / sit) *in a café with Mom.* (4) ______ (she / love) *Barcelona.* (5) ______ (she / come) *here every year.* (6) ______ (Dad / shop) *right now. He's sad because Barcelona Football Club* (7) ______ (not / play) *here this week. How are things at home?* (8) ______ (you / do) *all the household chores?*

Jenny

20 Barcelona

___ /16

Present progressive for future arrangements

4 Put Harry's words in order to make a phone conversation.

Jenny: Hello?
Harry: Harry. / Hello. / It's
(1) ______
Jenny: Harry? Is everything OK? Why are you calling me?
Harry: you / home? / When / coming / are
(2) ______
Jenny: We're flying home on Saturday. Why?
Harry: to / going / tonight. / back / factory / the / am / I
(3) ______
Jenny: Why, Harry?
Harry: problems. / are / some / fixing / They
(4) ______
Jenny: Can you say that again? The connection is bad.
Harry: is / tomorrow. / starting / robot / work / Another
(5) ______
Jenny: Harry? You're breaking up. I can't hear you.
Harry: arriving / at / He's / 9 a.m. / His / too. / Harry / is / name (6) ______

___ /12

Your score: ___ /50

SKILLS CHECK

✓✓✓ Yes, I can. No problem!
✓✓ Yes, I can. But I need little help.
✓ Yes, I can. But I need a lot of help.

I can understand the main ideas when I read. ______
I can understand a situation when I listen. ______
I can help identify the cause of a problem. ______
I can check that I understand on the phone. ______
I can use *and*, *also*, and *too*. ______

Workbook, pages 106–107

READ

1 Read the text and the questions below. For each question, choose A, B, C, or D.

The *Family Solutions* app – a great solution

607 Ratings

BUY NOW!

Do you argue with your parents about clearing the table or washing the dishes, making your bed or cleaning your room? Do your parents find it hard to understand that you use social networking sites or hang out with friends all the time? If you can't see their point of view, then our new *Family Solutions* app can help.

With the *Family Solutions* app, teenagers and parents look at typical family arguments from both sides – and find a good solution. The app gives you tips and helps you make better choices, but it also helps your parents see situations from your point of view.

How does it work? You read different kinds of problems and then choose an answer from different options. The app explains why one answer is the best and why the other answers aren't so good.

Just imagine this situation: you're getting ready to go out with friends, but your parents want you to visit your grandparents. Do you say "We always go there on the weekend. I'm meeting my friends today," or do you say "OK, we can go there today, but I'd like to hang out with my friends tomorrow"? The first option doesn't make your parents or you feel good – but the second option makes everybody happy.

You can buy the *Family Solutions* app in the App Store. You can also find the *Family Solutions* app online – just type "Family Solutions App" into your web browser and then follow the instructions on the screen.

1 What does the text do?
   A It tells a funny story about an app.
   B It explains how to make an app.
   C It tries to sell an app.
   D It says if an app is good or bad.

2 Who is the app for?
   A teenagers
   B parents of teenagers
   C parents and teenagers
   D parents and grandparents

3 What does "argument" mean?
   A a family party
   B a discussion between people with different opinions
   C to talk about something in front of the class
   D a friendly chat with family members

4 How does the app work?
   A You choose an answer for a situation.
   B You think of a lot of problems.
   C You play a card game.
   D You find information about your family online.

5 Which of the following is the best description of the app?
   A It finds a solution for all of life's problems.
   B It gives families ideas for new free-time activities.
   C It helps families understand each other better.
   D It explains how to make your family angry.

TEST-TAKING TIPS

answer multiple-choice questions

- Read all the questions carefully and then read the text.
- Read each question again and read all the choices.
- Decide which choices are definitely wrong.
- Look at the text again to help you choose the correct answer.

Reading: ______ /10

LISTEN

2 30 **Listen and check (✓) the correct picture for each question.**

1 How much is the computer?

A ☐

B ☐

C ☐

2 Where is Danny?

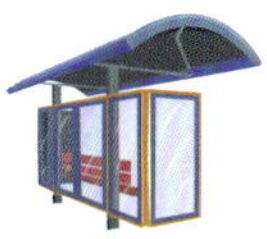
A ☐

B ☐

C ☐

3 Where are the speakers and what are they talking about?

A ☐

B ☐

C ☐

4 What are the girls doing tomorrow afternoon?

A ☐

B ☐

C ☐

5 Which instrument does the boy want to play?

A ☐

B ☐
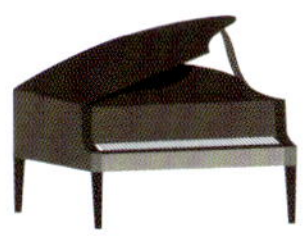
C ☐

Listening: _______ /10

WRITE

3 Complete the second sentence so that it means the same as the first. Use no more than three words.

1 I read a book two or three times a year.
I hardly .... books.

2 I watch online videos after school every day.
I .... online videos after school.

3 My mom teaches math.
My mom .... math teacher.

4 I have an arrangement to meet my friend tomorrow.
I'm .... my friend tomorrow.

_______ /4

4 Write a message to your new online friend Angelo about your free-time activities (35–45 words).

- Tell Angelo about at least three of your free-time activities.
- Say how often you do these activities and when you do them.
- Ask Angelo what activities he does and how often he does them.

_______ /6

Writing: _______ /10

Progress check score _______ /30

TEST-TAKING TIPS

answer multiple-choice questions with pictures

- Read the questions carefully before you listen.
- Look at the pictures: what English words and numbers do they show?
- Listen carefully to these words and numbers, and for the main ideas.
- When you listen again, check your answers.

TEST-TAKING TIPS

do sentence transformations

- Read the instructions. How many words can you use?
- Read both sentences carefully.
- Decide if the missing words are nouns, verbs, or another part of speech.
- Check that the meaning is the same and your spelling is correct.

write a short message or blog post

- Read the task carefully.
- Include the three things in the task.
- Use the correct tenses: past, present, and future.
- Use the correct number of words – count them.

UNIT 3

WILD WORLD

IN THE PICTURE The natural world

Talk about landscapes and natural features

WORK WITH WORDS

1 RECALL Work in pairs. Complete the words with vowels (a, e, i, o, u). Use the photos to help you. You have one minute.

1 b _e_ _a_ c h
2 ___ s l ___ n d
3 m ___ ___ n t ___ ___ n
4 r ___ v ___ r
5 ___ c ___ ___ n
6 t r ___ ___

2 31 Find these things in the photos. Then listen and repeat.

1 coast _c_
2 desert ___
3 forest ___
4 ice sheet ___
5 lake ___
6 savannah ___

3 Use the words in Exercise 2 to complete the sentences.

1 The Taiga is the largest _forest_ in the world.
2 Ninety Mile Beach is on the southeastern ___ of Australia.
3 The Sahara is the second largest ___ in the world.
4 The Serengeti ___ is in Africa.
5 Crater ___ is the deepest ___ in the USA.
6 A giant ___ covers Antarctica.

4 Read the clues and write the name of the places from Exercise 3.

1 From end to end it's 151 kilometers long. _Ninety Mile Beach_
2 The island on the west side of the lake is called Wizard Island. ___
3 It has the lowest temperature on Earth. ___
4 The name means "the great desert." ___
5 It inspired the movie *The Lion King*. ___
6 It has a third of all the trees in the world. ___

5 THE MOVING PICTURE Watch the video and check your answers to Exercises 3 and 4.

6 32 Match the words to the letters in the picture. Then listen and repeat.

countryside _c_
field ___
flower ___
grass ___
hill ___
stream ___

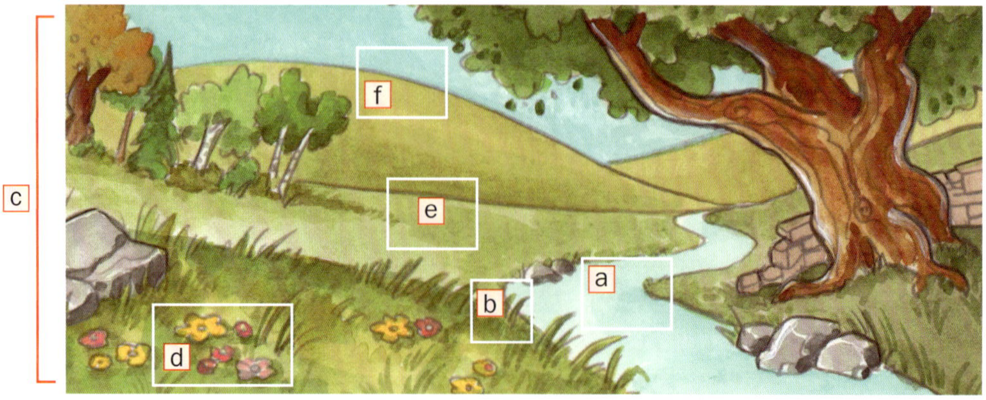

d

e

f

7 33 **Complete the description of the picture from Exercise 6. Then listen and check.**

The (1) *countryside* near my home is very beautiful. I often go to a big (2) .... and lie down on the (3) .... I close my eyes and listen to the water in the (4) .... and smell the (5) .... Sometimes I walk up the (6) .... to look at the view.

SPEAK

8 **Work in pairs. Think of a natural feature in your country or a place near your home. Describe the place to your partner. Can he or she draw a picture of the place you describe?**

MOVE BEYOND

Do the Words & Beyond exercise on page 71.

PHRASE BYTES

There are some mountains …

… is beside a river …

Next to the beach there's a …

Workbook, page 108

READING An environmental superstar

>>> Find specific information

SPEAK

1 Work in pairs. Answer the questions.

1 How often do you give presentations to your class? What was the last one about?
2 Do you like speaking in front of other people? Why or why not?

PHRASE BYTES

I hardly ever / often give presentations.
The last presentation was about …
I like / don't mind / hate speaking in public because …

READ

2 Look at the title of the article and the photo. Can you guess the answer to these questions?

1 How old is the boy?
2 Where is he?
3 What's he doing there?
4 What exactly does he want people to do?

Do you have the Felix Factor?

When Felix Finkbeiner was 13 years old, he made a speech at the United Nations in New York. He spoke in English and his message was simple – save the world's forests. How did a boy from Germany become "an environmental superstar"?

The story starts in 2007 when Felix did a project on climate change at his elementary school in Starnberg, near Munich in Germany. He saw some information online about Wangari Maathai, a Kenyan woman. She started a tree-planting campaign in 1977 and won the Nobel Peace Prize in 2004. Felix thought her campaign was interesting, and he decided to talk about it in class.

His presentation was a success, and he gave the same presentation to other classes. Two months later, Felix planted his first tree and started a campaign to plant a million trees. He called his campaign "Plant for the Planet."

Students at other schools joined the campaign. Together they planted 50,000 trees in Germany. They made a website for the campaign, and soon other countries began taking part. They wanted to meet Felix, so he started to give presentations outside the country. In November 2008, he spoke to the European Parliament.

At the beginning of 2011, the International Year of Forests, Felix made his speech at the United Nations. He asked world leaders to "stop talking – start planting." In the same year, his campaign reached its goal of planting one million trees in Germany. He also traveled to Kenya and met Wangari Maathai. And it all began with a school project.

3 a Read the tips in the HOW TO box.

b 34 Read the article quickly to check or find the answers to the questions in Exercise 2.

HOW TO

find specific information

- [ ] Don't read the entire text first.
- [ ] Read the start of each paragraph. Does it have the information you need? If not, read the next paragraph.
- [ ] Look for words connected to the information you need.

4 Which tips in the HOW TO box did you use for help with Exercise 3b? Check (✓) them.

5 Read the article and put these events in order.

___ Students created a website for Felix's campaign.
___ Felix gave a presentation to his class.
___ Felix spoke at the United Nations.
___ People from other countries joined his campaign.
___ Felix started a tree-planting campaign.
1 Felix read about a Kenyan woman's campaign.

MOVE BEYOND

What verb comes before these words in the article?

a speech, a project, the Nobel Prize, the same presentation, a campaign, 50,000 trees

REACT

6 Work in pairs. What do you think? Tell your partner.

1 What do you think about Felix's campaign?
2 Do you want to join his campaign? Why or why not?

Workbook, page 109

GRAMMAR Simple past

»» Describe completed events in the past

READ »» Grammar in context

1 Read the conversation. Why is Severn famous?

Jan: This is Severn Cullis-Suzuki. She talked at the United Nations' Earth Summit in 1992. She was only twelve.
Steve: Was she on TV?
Jan: Yes, she was, but I didn't see her. I saw the video later. She told adults to stop destroying the environment and create a better world.
Steve: Did she look nervous?
Jan: No, she didn't. She wasn't nervous at all.

STUDY

2 Complete the explanations and examples. Use Exercise 1 to help you.

Simple past

Use the simple past for completed actions in the past.

Regular past verbs add ________ to the base verb.
She talked at the United Nations.

Irregular past verbs change in form. See page 140.
I ________ the video later.

Negative past action verbs use ________ + base verb.
I didn't see her.

Questions and short answers with action verbs use *did* or *didn't*.
________ she look nervous? No, she ________.

Questions and short answers with *to be* use *was, wasn't, were, or weren't.*
________ she on TV? Yes, she ________.

See GRAMMAR DATABASE, page 66.

PRACTICE

3 Complete the sentences with the simple past form of the verbs.

1 Severn Cullis-Suzuki's father *taught* (teach) genetics at a university in Canada.
2 He ________ (be) also an environmental activist and TV reporter.
3 Severn ________ (become) an environmental activist in elementary school.
4 She ________ (start) ECO, an environmental organization, at the age of nine.
5 When they ________ (be) 12, four members of ECO ________ (travel) to the United Nations' Earth Summit in Brazil.
6 They ________ (buy) their plane tickets with the money that they ________ (make) from ECO activities.

»» Workbook, pages 110–111

4 a ▶35 PRONOUNCE **Listen to the simple past verbs. Underline the /ɔ/ sound.**

saw thought talked taught bought

b ▶36 **Listen and repeat the verbs. Pay attention to the /ɔ/ sound.**

5 Complete the biography with the simple past form of the verbs.

Wangari Maathai was born in Kenya in 1940. She (1) *started* (start) elementary school when she (2) ________ (be) eight. She (3) ________ (be) at the top of her class when she (4) ________ (finish) middle school. She then (5) ________ (go) to one of the only high schools for girls in Kenya. After high school she (6) ________ (study) biology at a university in the USA and then (7) ________ (get) a master's degree. In 1977, she (8) ________ (begin) the Green Belt Movement. It organizes women in rural Kenya to plant trees. In 2004, she (9) ________ (win) the Nobel Peace Prize. Wangari (10) ________ (die) in 2011.

6 Correct the sentences about Wangari Maathai.

1 Wangari Maathai was American.
She wasn't American. She was Kenyan.
2 There were a lot of high schools for girls in Kenya.
____
3 She studied history at a university.
____
4 She started the Green Tree Movement.
____
5 Wangari won the Nobel Prize for Literature.
____

7 Write questions in the simple past.

1 What / the name of your first school?
What was the name of your first school?
2 How old / you / when you started there?
____
3 you / like your first school?
____
4 When / you / start middle school?
____
5 Who / your first new friend in middle school?
____

SPEAK

8 Work in pairs. Use the questions in Exercise 7 to interview your partner about his or her early school years.

››› Take notes

SPEAK AND LISTEN

1 Work in pairs. Tell your partner how often you take photos and what you take photos of.

2 Look at the photo website and the three photos. Where are the snake, the penguins, and the ants?

Do you have a wonderful wildlife photo?
What was the animal doing when you took the photo?

Upload your photo here and record your story.

Frog for dinner?

A penguin family

Ant teamwork

3 a Read the tips in the HOW TO box.

b 37 Listen and take notes about the three photos in Exercise 2. Think of *Where? When? What?* Listen again and complete your notes. Compare in pairs.

4 Which tips in the HOW TO box did you use for help with Exercise 3b? Check (✓) them.

HOW TO
take notes

- ☐ Only write the most important words and ideas.
- ☐ Use symbols – ☺ for *great/fantastic*, ☹ for *terrible*, & for *and*.
- ☐ Don't worry about spelling and grammar. You can check later.

REACT

5 Work in pairs. Tell your partner which photo you like best and why. How did it make you feel?

WORK WITH WORDS

6 a 38 Look at the photos of wildlife. Listen and repeat.

b 39 Listen to the sounds and guess the animal. Which animals don't have a sound?

7 Work in pairs. Write lists using the words to the right. Do you know more animals? Add them.

Land and water animals *frog*
Birds ....
Insects ....
Reptiles ....

1 ant

2 bear

3 bee

4 crocodile

5 dolphin

6 turtle

7 frog

8 owl

9 parrot

10 penguin

11 snake

12 spider

MOVE BEYOND
Do the Words & Beyond exercise on page 71.

››› Workbook, pages 112–113

GRAMMAR Past progressive and simple past

>>> Talk about actions in progress and finished actions in the past

READ >>> Grammar in context

1 Look at the photo and read the story. What is the man in the photo "wearing"? Why?

While I was visiting a festival in the countryside last summer, I saw something very strange. In the afternoon I was getting a little bored, when I heard something about a "bee beard" competition. I went to look. There were seven or eight people in the competition, and hundreds of bees were sitting on their faces, necks, and shoulders. The bees weren't hurting them. The judge weighed the people while the bees were sitting on them. The person with the most bees won the competition.

STUDY

2 Complete the examples. Use Exercise 1 to help you.

Past progressive

Use the past progressive for actions in progress in the past.

Affirmative and negative forms

Use *I, he, she, it* + *was (not)* + verb + *-ing*.
Use *you, we, they* + *were (not)* + verb + *-ing*.

I ______ attending a festival in the park.
He ______ planning to go to the bee competition.

Questions and short answers

Use *was* or *were* + subject + verb + *-ing*

______ the bees hurting the people?
No, they ______.

Don't use the past progressive with verbs that describe the senses, thinking, or feeling.

See GRAMMAR DATABASE, page 66.

3 Complete the explanations with the correct tense.

Past progressive or simple past

Use the ______ for actions in progress in the past.

Use the ______ for actions that interrupt an action in progress.
While I was attending a festival, I saw something strange.

Use the ______ after *while*.
The judge weighed the people while the bees were sitting on them.

Use the ______ after *when*.
I was leaving the festival when I saw a sign about a bee competition.

See GRAMMAR DATABASE, page 66.

PRACTICE

4 Complete the conversation with the past progressive form of the verbs.

Paz: What (1) were you doing (you / do) when you took this photo?
Alice: Well, it was 10 p.m. but I (2) ______ (not sleep). My sister and I (3) ______ (watch) an owl from our window. It (4) ______ (fly) in the sky. We were very quiet. We (5) ______ (not talk), and we (6) ______ (not move).
Paz: (7) ______ (the owl / hold) something?
Alice: Yes, it was. Maybe it (8) ______ (carry) a mouse or a frog.

5 Work in pairs. Ask and answer questions with your partner about what you were doing at different times yesterday.

What were you doing yesterday at 7 a.m. / 10 a.m. / 10 p.m.?
I was watching TV.
Were you sleeping at … ?
Yes, I was. / No, I wasn't. I was …

6 Choose the correct options to complete the story.

I live near the beach in New Zealand. One day I (1) *was fishing* / *fished* with my brother. While we (2) *were standing* / *stood* in the ocean, we (3) *were seeing* / *saw* something black near us. What was it? We (4) *weren't knowing* / *didn't know*. It (5) *was swimming* / *swam* toward us while we (6) *were watching* / *watched* it. It came closer and closer. We (7) *were getting* / *got* really scared until we (8) *were realizing* / *realized* it was only a dolphin.

WRITE AND SPEAK

7 Student A looks at the monkey photo on page 75. Student B looks at the elephant photo on page 76.

Make notes for a short story about your photo: *Where were you? When was it? What was the animal doing? What happened?* Show your photo to a partner. Tell him or her the story about it.

LANGUAGE & BEYOND

››› Use mind maps to organize information for a speech

READ

1 **Work in pairs. Answer the question.**

How do you usually remember information?

2 **Ryan is making a mind map to plan a school speech about bees. Write the missing words on the red lines.**

description problem what

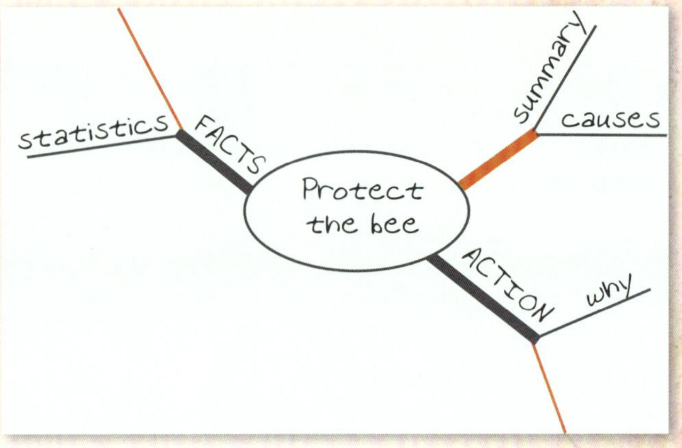

3 **Read Ryan's notes and match each point (1–6) to a thinner branch on the mind map.**

1 There are nearly 20,000 species.
2 Create a bee-friendly garden with plants and flowers.
3 The number of bees in the world is going down every year.
4 Bees are flying insects. They are usually yellow and black.
5 Experts do not know exactly what is causing the problem.
6 We need honey bees for one-third of our food.

DO

4 a **Read the tips for making a mind map.**

- Start with a main word or picture. Draw lines from the word or picture.
- Lines start thicker and become thinner, like branches on a tree.
- Write one or two key words on each line.
- Use CAPITAL LETTERS for important words.
- Use different colors, symbols, and images to make things clear.

b **Copy Ryan's mind map in your own style. Then add lines and key words for the information in Exercise 3.**

REFLECT

5 **Discuss the questions with your class. Do you agree with the REFLECTION POINT?**

1 What are the good things about mind maps?
2 What do you like / not like about mind maps?

REFLECTION POINT
Using a mind map helps you organize and remember information with your own words and pictures.

EXTEND

6 **You need to give a speech to your class. Work in groups. Choose one of the topics below. Create a mind map to organize your ideas.**

Litter in my neighborhood
Learning English
Keeping pets in cities
Cell phones

GET ORGANIZED

››› Workbook, page 117

Make and react to suggestions

SPEAK

1 **Your school wants to organize a Save the Planet Day, with activities connected to the environment. Work in pairs. Make a list of ideas.**

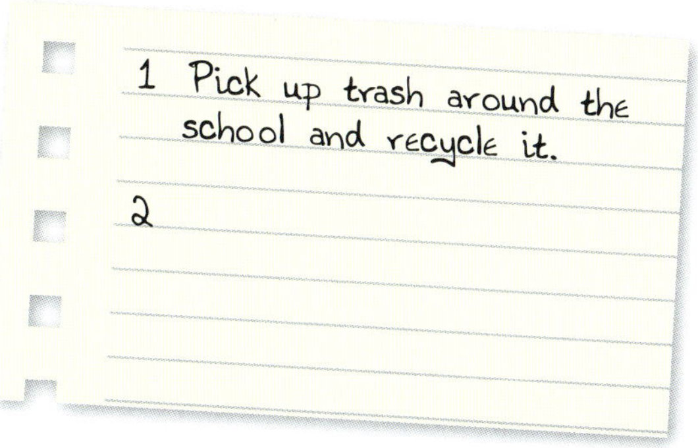

LISTEN

2 40 **Listen to the conversation. What ideas do the students have for Save the Planet Day? Are they on your list?**

Lucia: (1) Hey. ______ do for Save the Planet Day next month?
Carl: (2) ______ wear green clothes to school – green socks or a green hat.
Rick: No way! I'm not going to wear green.
Lucia: (3) ______ all walk to school?
Carl: Yes. Or ride our bikes here.
Rick: I don't know. I live really far away and I don't have a bike. Let's do a survey and ask people their opinions about the environment.
Lucia: That's pretty serious. (4) ______ making something from recycled materials?
Rick: That's a nice idea.
Carl: Yes, but it doesn't really help the environment. (5) ______ we do to really make a difference?
Lucia: I know! (6) ______ collect money for Save the Dolphins.
Carl: That's a great idea!

3 40 **Complete the conversation with the phrases in the box. Then listen again and check.**

We could	We could	What about	What could
What should we	Why don't we		

4 41 **Listen and repeat the sentences from the conversation.**

5 42 **Decide if the reactions are positive (*P*) or negative (*N*). Then listen and repeat the reactions.**

1 No way! P/N
2 I don't know. P/N
3 That's pretty serious. P/N
4 That's a nice idea. P/N
5 That's a great idea! P/N

ACT

6 **You are deciding what to do for a Save the Planet Day at your school. Work in pairs. Prepare a conversation. Include at least three suggestions and choose one.**

7 **Present your conversation to another pair, or to the class.**

PHRASEBOOK 43

Make suggestions

What should we do?
What could we make / wear?
We could make / wear …
Let's do / organize …
Why don't we walk / ride … ?
What / How about doing / making … ?

React to suggestions

No way!
I don't know.
That's pretty serious / not very exciting.
That's a nice / great / bad / terrible idea.

Workbook, page 115

WRITING A vacation story

»» Write a story with time expressions

SPEAK AND READ

1 Work in groups. Answer the questions.

1 Do you keep a diary or journal? Why or why not?
2 What kinds of things do people write about in diaries?

2 Read the diary entry. Why didn't Lynn sleep well?

JANUARY
Friday 4

Dear Diary,
Yesterday we arrived in Utah for our camping vacation in the desert. I'm feeling really tired today because something scary happened during the night. I was sleeping when a strange noise woke me up. At first I thought it was raining. But then I realized it was coming from inside the tent. After a minute or two, the noise stopped and I went back to sleep. Later I woke up again. This time something was moving inside my sleeping bag. I screamed and jumped out. Now everybody was awake. Mom got a flashlight and looked inside the sleeping bag and found a field mouse!

3 a Read the tips in the HOW TO box.

HOW TO
use time expressions

- Use time expressions like *yesterday afternoon*, *last night*, and *during the night* to say when things happened.
- Use *at first* to mean "in the beginning."
- Use *then* to say what happened next.
- Use *after* + a time period (*a minute or two*) to say time passes between two things.
- Use *later* to say something happened after another time or event.

b Underline examples of each time expression in the diary entry.

PRACTICE

4 Complete the description with expressions from the HOW TO box.

Something really scary happened (1) *yesterday* afternoon. I was riding my bike through the forest when I saw a dog. (2) ______ it looked really friendly, but a few seconds (3) ______ it started barking loudly. (4) ______ it ran toward me. I was really scared, so I turned around and rode away. (5) ______ about five minutes the dog stopped chasing me. (6) ______ in the afternoon I saw a man walking the dog, and it looked really friendly again.

DISCUSS

5 Describe some problems that might happen on a camping trip.

WRITE

6 Write a story about a camping trip.

1 Imagine one of the problems you discussed happened to you. Answer the questions: Where were you? When did you go? Who was with you? What were you doing?
2 Use the past progressive and simple past tense. Describe what you were doing and the problem that interrupted you.
3 Use time expressions to say when events happened. Put the events in the order they happened. See the HOW TO box.

SHARE

7 Take turns reading your new stories. Listen to your classmates. Who has a scary story, a funny story, or a strange story?

»» Workbook, pages 116–117

VOCABULARY Landscapes and natural features

1 Choose the correct options.

Wild World Vacations.com

See Greenland's huge (1) *desert* / *ice sheet* – it covers 80 percent of the country. Visit the small towns by the ocean along the island's (2) *coast* / *lake*.

Go on safari to the African (3) *forest* / *savannah* with its long (4) *hill* / *grass* and trees, and see amazing wildlife.

Large rivers and small (5) *streams* / *fields* flow into the Great (6) *Deserts* / *Lakes* of North America. Take a boat trip and relax.

Visit England, famous for its beautiful (7) *ice sheet* / *countryside* and its green (8) *flowers* / *fields*.

Death Valley in the Mojave (9) *Coast* / *Desert* is a very hot, dry place. But there are many beautiful (10) *streams* / *flowers* and plants here.

Stay in a traditional Spanish village on a (11) *savannah* / *hill* in Andalucia and go walking among the trees in the (12) *desert* / *forest*.

___ /12

Wildlife

2 Read the descriptions of wildlife and write the correct words.

See Australia's Wildlife

Land and water animals

1 This smart animal lives in the ocean. d ______
2 This scary animal usually lives in forests. b ______
3 This animal is green and can swim. f ______
4 This animal has eight legs. s ______

Insects

5 This insect is black and yellow. b ______
6 Thousands of these live together. a ______

Birds

7 This bird can learn to talk. p ______
8 It lives in Antarctica. p ______
9 This is a night bird. o ______

Reptiles

10 It's long and thin and makes a "sss" noise. s ______
11 This big reptile has dangerous teeth. c ______
12 This reptile usually lives in the ocean. t ______

___ /12

GRAMMAR Simple past

3 Complete the conversation with the simple past form of the verbs.

Lucy: Where (1) ______ (you / go) on vacation last year?
Sam: We (2) ______ (not go) anywhere last year. Two years ago we (3) ______ (stay) in a hotel in Greece for two weeks.
Lucy: Nice!
Sam: Well, the hotel (4) ______ (have) a great pool. I (5) ______ (love) it. We (6) ______ (go) swimming every day. But one day I (7) ______ (get) out of the water very fast. The pool was full of frogs!

___ /14

Past progressive and simple past

4 Complete the story with the past progressive or the simple past form of the verbs.

While we (1) ______ (visit) California with Wild World Vacations, we went for a walk in Yosemite National Park. We were walking down a hill when we (2) ______ (see) a big black bear. It (3) ______ (eat) something, and it (4) ______ (not look) at us. We (5) ______ (stop) walking and didn't move. While we (6) ______ (stand) there, it moved away.

___ /12

Your score: ___ /50

SKILLS CHECK

✓✓✓ Yes, I can. No problem!
✓✓ Yes, I can. But I need a little help.
✓ Yes, I can. But I need a lot of help.

I can find specific information when I read. ______
I can take notes when I listen. ______
I can use mind maps to organize information. ______
I can make and react to suggestions. ______
I can write a story with time expressions. ______

Workbook, pages 118–119

UNIT 4 WHAT'S COOKING?

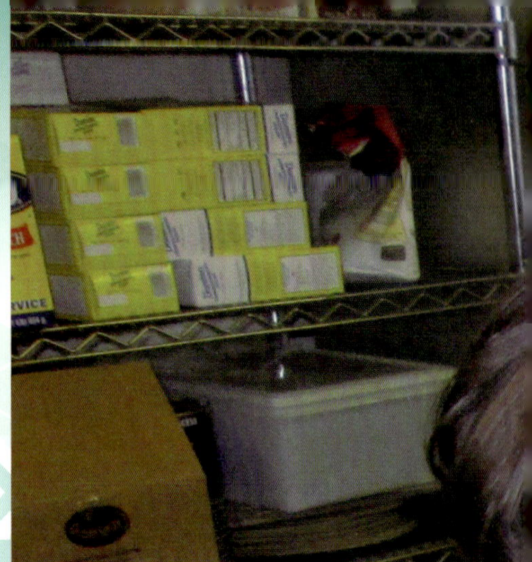

IN THE PICTURE Inside the kitchen

Talk about food and cooking

WORK WITH WORDS

1 RECALL **Work in pairs. Write lists of food words under the headings. You have three minutes.**

Vegetables	Fruit	Meat & Fish	Dairy	Other	Drinks
onion	*lemon*	*chicken*	*milk*	*bread*	*orange juice*

2 44 **Listen and order the photos.**

1 ____ 2 ____ 3 ____ 4 ____ 5 ____

3 45 **Find these things in the photos. Listen and repeat.**

1 a saucepan *b*
2 a frying pan ____
3 a bowl ____
4 a cutting board ____ ____ ____
5 a knife ____ ____

4 46 **Listen and repeat the words.**

beat chop cut fry heat pour stir

5 47 **Use words from Exercises 3 and 4 to complete the sentences. Then listen and check.**

So first you beat the eggs in a large (1) *bowl* like this.
After that, you (2) ____________ an onion – carefully. Don't forget to do it on a (3) ____________ .
Then you heat some oil in a (4) ____________ and (5) ____________ the chicken.
You (6) ____________ the lemon juice into a (7) ____________ and stir slowly.
Now, with a (8) ____________ you cut some bread.

6 a Work in pairs. Match the verbs in Exercise 4 to some of the words on your food list in Exercise 1.

Chop tomatoes.

Beat eggs.

b Work in pairs. Mime some of the actions. Can your partner say the correct phrases?

7 THE MOVING PICTURE **Watch the video. Would you like to go to Passport NYC? Why or why not?**

a

b

c

d

e

SPEAK

8 In pairs, read the advertisement and answer the questions.

1 What is a "foodie"? Are you a foodie?
2 What is your favorite food?
3 Which of these things can you do: chop an onion, fry an egg, make a salad?

MOVE BEYOND

Do the Words & Beyond exercise on page 72.

Workbook, page 120

READING Zach's favorite recipe

Use headings to find specific information

SPEAK AND READ

1 Work in pairs. Answer the questions.

1 How often do you cook?
2 Are there any recipe books in your home? Do you use recipes? Why or why not?

2 a Read the tips in the HOW TO box.

b Look at the recipe. In which sections can you find the following information?

1 How do I make it?
2 How long does it take?
3 What things do I need?
4 Is it hard?

3 Which tips in the HOW TO box did you use for help with Exercise 2b? Check (✓) them.

HOW TO

use headings to find specific information

- ☐ Decide what information you need.
- ☐ Read the headings (and first sentence if necessary).
- ☐ Find the correct heading and read the information under this heading.

Zach's Spanish Omelette

Level of difficulty	Time	Serves
easy	40 minutes	four people

ABOUT THIS RECIPE

I love food, but I don't have much time to cook. This is one of my favorite recipes because there aren't many ingredients and it doesn't need a lot of preparation. All you need are some potatoes, an onion, a few eggs, and some oil. It's easy. Try it and see.

Ingredients

500 g potatoes
one onion
150 ml oil
six eggs

TIP
Don't cut the omelette when it's very hot. Wait for it to cool (about 10 minutes).

Directions

1 Cut the potatoes into small pieces. Chop the onion.
2 Heat the oil in a large frying pan. Add the potatoes and onion and fry for 20–30 minutes. Stir occasionally until the potatoes are soft.
3 Beat the eggs in a bowl.
4 Add the potatoes and onions to the bowl and stir with the eggs. Before you pour the mixture into the frying pan, add some salt and pepper. Then cook on medium heat.
5 To cook the top of the omelette, put the frying pan under the broiler for a few minutes. Or turn the omelette in the frying pan.

ZACH'S FOOD FACTS

Many countries have their own kinds of omelette. The Italian frittata contains cheese, vegetables, and sometimes pasta. A Chinese omelette has vegetables and soy sauce. There are peppers and hot chilies in a Mexican omelette. The classic French omelette has … eggs! Do you know any egg recipes?

4 48 Read the recipe again to decide if each statement is correct (*C*) or incorrect (*I*).

1 You can make the omelette in under an hour. *C*
2 Leave the omelette to cool before cutting it. ____
3 Add salt and pepper when you beat the eggs. ____
4 You need three different vegetables to make the omelette. ____
5 A Chinese omelette has vegetables and pasta. ____
6 The chef likes the recipe because it's quick to make. ____

MOVE BEYOND

Work in pairs. Close your books and explain the recipe to each other. How much can you remember?

REACT

5 Work in pairs. What do you think? Tell your partner.

1 It's a good/bad recipe because …
2 After reading the recipe I think / don't think I can make a Spanish omelette.
3 I know some / don't know any egg recipes.

Workbook, page 121

GRAMMAR Expressions of quantity

Talk about quantity

READ AND LISTEN Grammar in context

1 49 **Read and listen to the conversation. Which omelette can Tanya and Leo make for lunch – Spanish, Italian, Chinese, or Mexican? (See the recipe on page 44 to help you.)**

Tanya: There isn't much food. There are a few eggs. And there's some pasta – about half a package.
Leo: How many eggs are there?
Tanya: Three. And there's a little cheese too – but not much.
Leo: Is there any bread?
Tanya: No, there's no bread. But there are a lot of vegetables.

STUDY

2 Complete the table with the words in the box. Use Exercise 1 to help you.

large quantity   not large or small quantity
small quantity   zero

Expressions of quantity

Expression of quantity	Quantity
a lot of	......
some	......
a few, a little, not much, not many	......
no	......

See GRAMMAR DATABASE, page 67.

3 Look at the table. Which expression can you use before all nouns and in all kinds of sentences?

Countable and uncountable

	Countable *egg(s)*	Uncountable *pasta*
+	*some, no* *a few, a lot of*	*some, no* *a little, a lot of*
–	*any, many, a lot of*	*any, much, a lot of*
?	*any, many* *a few, a lot of*	*any, much* *a little, a lot of*

See GRAMMAR DATABASE, page 67.

PRACTICE

4 Write short descriptions. Use the words in the box.

a few   a little   a lot of   no   ~~some~~

1 *some* bread

2 ...... vegetables

3 ...... apples

4 ...... pasta

5 ...... rice

5 Choose the correct options.

I'm not a very good cook because I don't have (1) *much* / *many* time. During the week I don't make (2) *any* / *no* meals except breakfast. I usually have (3) *a* / *some* toast and a (4) *few* / *little* orange juice. On the weekend I sometimes help make lunch, but I don't know (5) *much* / *many* good recipes so I just follow my big sister's instructions. She's a great cook and she makes (6) *many* / *a lot of* really nice food.

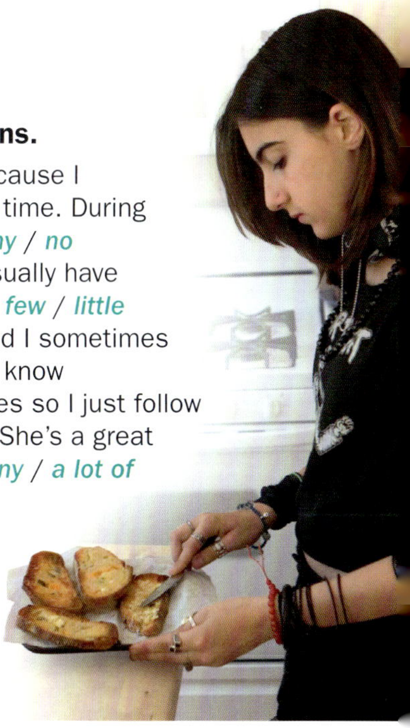

6 Complete the questions with one word.

1 You're hungry but you have *no* time to cook. What do you eat?
2 How ...... take-out food do you eat?
3 Do you hate ...... vegetables? Which ones? Which ones do you like?
4 A ...... friends are watching a movie at your house. What snacks do you offer them?
5 Do you eat a ...... of fruit? What's your favorite fruit?
6 You need to make ...... food for a picnic. What do you make?

SPEAK

7 Work in pairs. Answer the questions in Exercise 6. Who makes healthy choices?

Workbook, pages 122–123

LISTENING AND VOCABULARY What a waste!

Recognize facts and opinions

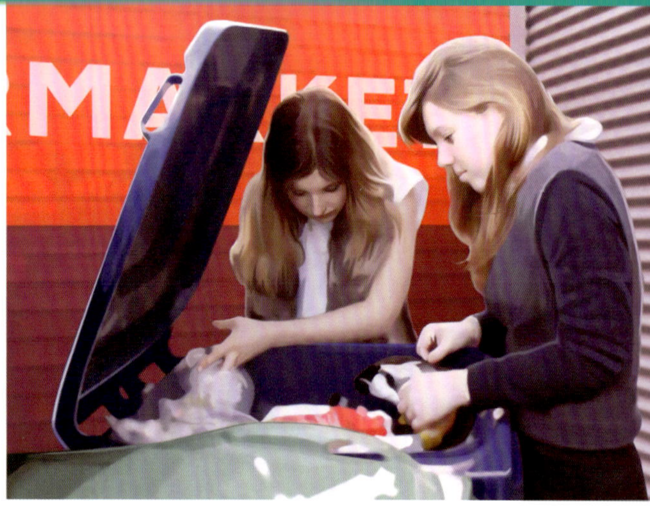

SPEAK AND LISTEN

1 Look at the picture. What do you think the people are doing? Choose A, B, or C.

A They're throwing leftover food in the trash can.
B They're looking at what the supermarket threw away.
C They lost something in the trash can, and now they're looking for it.

2 ▶50 Emma is one of the people in the picture. Listen to an interview with her and check your answer to Exercise 1. What's on her list?

3 a Read the tips in the HOW TO box.

b ▶50 Listen again. Which sentences are facts (*F*) in the interview? Which are opinions (*O*)?

1 Every year the world wastes a lot of food. *F*
2 Europe and North America waste 100 kg of food per person each year. ____
3 Supermarkets throw away a lot of food. ____
4 Supermarkets have to throw away all the food that they can't sell. ____
5 It's wrong to waste food. ____

HOW TO

recognize facts and opinions

☐ **Facts:** Listen for numbers and percentages (%).

☐ **Opinions:** Listen for phrases like *I think …* , *In my opinion …* , and for words meaning "good" or "bad" like *OK*, *wrong*.

4 Which tips in the HOW TO box did you use for help with Exercise 3b? Check (✓) them.

REACT

5 Work in pairs. What do you think? Tell your partner.

1 Is it wrong for supermarkets to throw away food?
2 Is it OK to take food from supermarket trash cans?

WORK WITH WORDS

6 ▶51 Match the phrases for containers and amounts to the pictures. Listen and check.

1 a bottle of water *a*
2 a box of chocolates ____
3 a package of pasta ____
4 a can of soda ____
5 a carton of milk ____
6 a jar of jam ____
7 a loaf of bread ____
8 a piece of meat ____

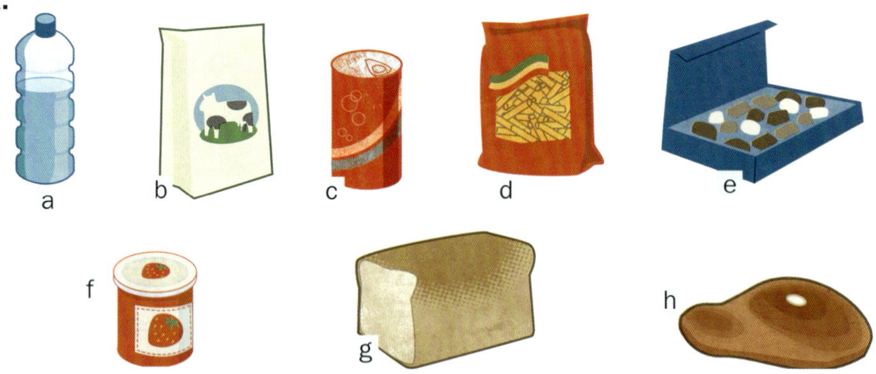

7 ▶52 PRONOUNCE Listen to the phrases in Exercise 6 again. Underline the words that aren't stressed. Then listen again and repeat phrases.

8 Look at the pictures in Exercise 6 then close your book. Make a list of what you remember. Check your list with a partner.

Is there a can of soup?

No, there's a can of soda.

MOVE BEYOND

Do the Words & Beyond exercise on page 72.

Workbook, pages 124–125

GRAMMAR Indefinite pronouns

››› Use indefinite pronouns

READ ››› Grammar in context

1 Read the facts. Which fact do you think is most interesting?

Nobody likes waste.
But nearly **everybody** wastes food.

FACT: Farmers **everywhere** throw away good fruit and vegetables. Why? Because supermarkets and food stores don't buy **anything** with a strange shape.

FACT: 24–35 percent of school lunches go in the trash. We can do **something** about this!

STUDY

2 Choose the correct option. Use Exercise 1 to help you.

Indefinite pronouns

Use indefinite pronouns to refer to a nonspecific person, thing, or place.

Use a third person **singular** / **plural** verb with all indefinite pronouns.
Nearly everybody wastes food.

Use *every-*, *no-* and ***some-*** / ***any-*** in affirmative sentences.
We can do something about this.
Nobody likes waste.

Use *any-* in questions and ***affirmative*** / ***negative*** sentences.
Supermarkets don't buy anything with a strange shape.

See GRAMMAR DATABASE, page 67.

3 Complete the table with indefinite pronouns.

People	Things	Places
somebody	something	somewhere
....	....	anywhere
....	everything	....
nobody	....	....

PRACTICE

4 a Complete the indefinite pronouns with *some*, *any*, *every*, or *no*.

Alex: (1) *No*body in my family wastes food. My parents always tell us to eat (2) ....thing on our plates.
Nate: Really? I often leave (3) ....thing when I don't like it. Why eat it?
Alex: Well, (4) ....body in my family is a great cook. I always like the food at home.
Nate: My parents are terrible cooks. They can't cook (5) ....thing! I love it when we eat out (6) ....where.

b Which sentences in Exercise 4a are true about you or your family?

5 Complete these tips with indefinite pronouns. What do you think of these ideas?

Do (1) *something* to stop food waste at school!

All of you! (2) .... can help.
Eat all your school lunch. Don't throw (3) .... away.
Does (4) .... in your class have a more interesting lunch box? Trade!
Or make lunch yourself, so you like (5) .... in it.
Does your school have a garden? Is there (6) .... to put leftover fruit and vegetables?

WRITE AND SPEAK

6 a Read the poem below. Do you like it? Why or why not?

b Write your poem. Use the words in color and the ideas in the cloud. Comment on your partner's poem.

is / isn't
likes / eats / wears /
has / hurts / helps /
fights / tells me
there is / there are

In my perfect world ...

Nobody is hungry.
Everybody smiles.
Nothing hurts.
Everything is peaceful.
Everywhere there are
happy faces.
(by *Laura, 15*)

››› Workbook, page 126

LANGUAGE & BEYOND

Asha ________________. She doesn't eat any meat or fish, but she eats dairy products like eggs, milk, and cheese.

Carmelo ________________ so he can't eat any food with them in it, especially cake and cookies.

Lucy ________________. That means she can't eat anything with flour in it, like bread, pasta, or pizza.

»» Consider other people's needs and preferences

RESPECT OTHERS

READ

1 A group of American students are visiting your school. Three of them have special diets. Read the information about them above and complete their profiles with the correct phrase.

can't eat gluten   is allergic to eggs   is a vegetarian

2 Work in pairs. Make a list of the food you can see in the photos. Then write A (Asha), C (Carmelo), or L (Lucy) next to the food they can't eat.

1

2

3

4

5

6

7

DO

3 Your class is organizing a party to welcome the group of American students.

- In groups, make a list of food for the party.
- Include options for Asha, Carmelo, and Lucy.
- Consider the needs and preferences of other students in your class.

PHRASE BYTES

Let's bring …
Why don't we make … ?
What could we bring for … ?
Do we have anything for … ?
We need something without … in it.

REFLECT

4 Discuss the questions with your class. Do you agree with the REFLECTION POINT?

1 Whose special diet was the hardest to consider – Asha's, Carmelo's, or Lucy's? Why?
2 Do you know anybody with a special diet? Describe it.
3 How do you think people with special diets feel when they can't eat anything at a meal or party?

REFLECTION POINT

It isn't always easy to consider other people's needs and preferences. But when you consider them, people feel better.

EXTEND

5 Work in groups. Make a music playlist for the welcome party. Think about the preferences of other people in your class.

Workbook, page 129

SPEAKING At a restaurant

Express preferences when you order food

SPEAK

1 Work in pairs. Answer the questions.

1 What kinds of restaurants are near your home or school?
2 What's your favorite meal when you eat in a restaurant?

LISTEN

2 53 Listen to the conversation. What do Rick and Sandy order? Complete the sentences.

Server: Hi. Are you ready to order?
Rick: Yes. I'd like the (1) *chicken sandwich*, please. Can I have it without onions?
Server: Of course. Would you like some fries with it?
Rick: No, thanks. I'd rather have (2) ______ .
Server: OK.
Sandy: I'd like the (3) ______ , please. And I'd prefer (4) ______ with it.
Server: OK. Would you like anything to drink?
Rick: Do you have any fresh orange juice?
Server: No, but we have milkshakes and sodas.
Rick: Um ... I'll have some (5) ______ .
Sandy: I'd like a (6) ______ , please.

3 a Read the tips in the HOW TO box.

b Write the polite versions of the sentences from the conversation in Exercise 2.

1 Give me a milkshake. *I'd like a milkshake, please.*
2 I don't want onions. ______
3 Drink? ______
4 I don't want fries, I want salad. ______
5 What do you want to eat? ______
6 Water! ______

HOW TO

be polite

- Use polite requests like *Can I have ... ?* and *I'd like ...*
- Say *please* and *thank you*.

ACT

OUR SPECIALS

Chef's Sandwich (chicken with onions, lettuce, and tomato)
Cheeseburger (100% beef burger with cheese, onions, and ketchup)
Spanish Omelette (eggs, potatoes, and onions)
Chef's Salad (lettuce, tomatoes, peppers, and eggs)

SIDE DISHES

Salad, Fries, or Fried Rice

DRINKS

Selection of delicious milkshakes and cool sodas.
Ask your server for today's specials.

4 Work in groups of three or four.

- Choose something you'd like to eat and drink from the menu.
- Choose one person in the group to be the server.
- The server takes the order. What do you say? Use the conversation in Exercise 2 to help you.

PHRASEBOOK 54

Order food

I'd like ...
I'll have ...
Can I have a / some ... ?
Do you have any ... ?

Express a preference

I'd rather have ...
I'd prefer (to have) ...

Workbook, page 127

WRITING My favorite recipe

Order ideas

SPEAK AND READ

1 Look at the photo in the recipe for pancakes. Would you like to eat this? Why or why not?

MY FAVORITE RECIPE: *pancakes*

Ingredients

225 g flour, a little salt, two eggs, 580 ml milk

Directions

- After that, pour in the milk and beat it with the flour and eggs.
- Finally, heat a little oil in a frying pan. Pour in some mixture and fry the pancakes on both sides until they're golden brown.
- Next, make a hole in the middle of the flour. Add the eggs and stir together with the flour.
- First, put the flour in a bowl with a little salt.
- Then leave the pancake mixture for 15–20 minutes.

MY TIP

Eat the pancakes as dessert with fruit and cream, chocolate sauce, or lemon juice and sugar.

PHRASE BYTES

Yes, it looks delicious!

No, I don't like fruit / sweet things.

No, I can't eat things with flour.

2 a Read the tips in the HOW TO box.

b Underline words to order ideas in the recipe.

HOW TO

order ideas

- Use *first* for step 1.
- Use *next*, *after that*, and *then* for the next steps (in any order).
- Use *finally* for the last step.

3 Read the recipe and put the directions in the correct order. Use the HOW TO box to help you.

PRACTICE

4 Use words from Exercise 2 to order the recipe for Black Bean and Corn Salad.

(1) *First*, chop some small tomatoes, an onion, and some cilantro. (2) ________ cut one small hot green chili. (3) ________ stir the tomatoes, the onion, the cilantro, a can of beans, and a can of corn in a bowl. (4) ________ mix some oil and lime juice with a little salt and pepper. (5) ________ pour it over the salad.

DISCUSS

5 Discuss a simple recipe that you know how to prepare.

WRITE

6 Write the recipe you discussed. Make a list of the ingredients. Write the quantity and the ingredient.

1. Use a number or a quantity: *three eggs*, *a little salt*.
2. Write the instructions. Use order words. Use *first*, *next*, *then*, *after that, and finally* to state the instructions. See the HOW TO box.
3. Include a tip. When do you like to eat this? How do you like to eat this? Is there a secret ingredient?

SHARE

7 Take turns reading your recipe. Listen to your classmates. Which recipe would you like to try?

Workbook, pages 128–129

VOCABULARY Kitchen equipment and cooking verbs

1 Choose the correct options to complete the instructions.

Phil: (1) *Chop* / *Stir* a large onion into small pieces. Use a big (2) *bowl* / *knife* and a (3) *cutting* / *frying* board. Then (4) *beat* / *fry* them in the (5) *cutting* / *frying* pan.

Sue: (6) *Cut* / *Heat* a liter of milk in a big (7) *knife* / *saucepan*. When it's hot, (8) *heat* / *pour* in the cake mix. Remember to (9) *fry* / *stir* all the time to mix it well.

Lynn: (10) *Beat* / *Chop* eight eggs in a (11) *bowl* / *saucepan*. Then (12) *cut* / *pour* some bread for sandwiches.

___ /12

Containers and amounts

2 Complete the words on the shopping list for a party.

A large onion
(1) A c ________ of milk
(2) A b ________ of cookies
(3) A j ________ of jam
(4) 2 c ________ of eggs
(5) 8 l ________ of French bread
(6) 8 p ________ of chicken
(7) 4 c ________ of fruit juice
(8) 12 c ________ of soda

___ /8

GRAMMAR Expressions of quantity

3 Complete the phone conversation with the words in the box.

any few little lot many much no some

Sue: Hi, Tom. Everything's ready for the party.
Tom: So how (1) ________ food is there?
Sue: Well, we've made a (2) ________ of sandwiches. About 30! There are a (3) ________ different omelettes too, (4) ________ pieces of spicy chicken, a big salad, cake, and a (5) ________ ice cream too, but not much.
Tom: Are there (6) ________ tomatoes in the salad? You know I hate tomatoes.
Sue: No, there are (7) ________ tomatoes in it. I remembered!
Tom: How (8) ________ people are coming?
Sue: About 15.
Tom: Great. See you at 6 p.m.

___ /16

Indefinite pronouns

4 Complete with the correct indefinite pronouns (__*body*, __*thing*, __*where*).

"OK, the party's over, so I want (1) ________ to help clean up this mess. (2) ________'s going home until the house is clean again. To start with, (3) ________ needs to take the food to the kitchen. Can the rest of you put (4) ________ else into this plastic bag and check that there's (5) ________ under the sofa? There's food (6) ________ in the kitchen too. And one more thing, does (7) ________ know where the cat is?"

___ /14

Your score: ___ /50

SKILLS CHECK

✓✓✓ Yes, I can. No problem!
✓✓ Yes, I can. But I need a little help.
✓ Yes, I can. But I need a lot of help.

I can use headings to find specific information. ________
I can recognize facts and opinions when I listen. ________
I can consider other people's needs and preferences. ________
I can express preferences when I order food. ________
I can order ideas when I write. ________

Workbook, pages 130–131

READ

1 The people below are going on a vacation together. You're organizing the vacation and want everybody to enjoy it. Read the descriptions of activities. Decide which activity would be the best match suitable for each person.

1 **Victor** loves being by the coast with his friends, but he hates going in the water because he didn't learn to swim when he was child. He doesn't like any sports or being active.

2 **Sienna** likes sports and outdoor games, especially water sports. Last year she learned to kayak at summer camp. She also loves animals.

3 **Salvatore** hates busy places where there are a lot of people. He likes being in the countryside. He's a good photographer, and last year he won a wildlife photography competition.

4 **Yoko** worries about environmental problems. Last month she organized a *Save Our Climate* campaign at school, and it was a great success. She's scared of swimming and insects.

5 **Ted** is a foodie and a fantastic cook. His parents bought a restaurant a few years ago, and he often helps in the kitchen. He thinks it's important to eat fresh, healthy food.

TEST-TAKING TIPS

do a matching exercise (people + texts)

- Read all the people profiles carefully.
- In the people profiles, underline important words or phrases.
- In the activity descriptions, look for ideas that match the important words.
- Make sure all the information about the people matches the description.

Vacation activities

A Forest visit

Learn about the different species of animals and flowers in the forest. Find out about the lives of ants, bees, owls, snakes, and spiders and how tourists are destroying their habitats. Small groups only and no loud music or phones.

B Walk by the ocean

A five-kilometer group walk along the beach. We'll tell you about the history of the area. Learn how important the ocean was for local people in the past when most people worked on fishing boats. Wear comfortable shoes and appropriate beach clothes.

C Cooking class

In this class, we cook very easy dishes with fresh local foods. Are you a beginner in the kitchen? Can't fry an egg or chop an onion? Can't even remember the last time you used a saucepan or a cutting board and knife? Then this class is for you!

D Tree planting

A great way to have a fun day but also do something for our world. Trees clean our air, but every year we cut down 3–6 billion to build houses and roads, to clear land for farms, and to make furniture. Help us plant new ones.

E Boat trip

Join us on an exciting boat trip on the ocean. During the two-hour stop on a small island, you can go swimming, diving, or water-skiing with our trained instructors. Maybe we'll see some turtles or dolphins somewhere on the trip. Good swimmers only.

F Market day

Visit the local market – it was Market of the Year this year. There are clothes, bags, shoes – everything you can think of. There's also a lot of food, of course – vegetables, meat, fruit, fish, cake, and bread … And the great thing is, you can try everything!

G Beach trip

Lie on the beach all afternoon! Listen to the sound of the ocean and dream. Or enter our sandcastle competition and make a big castle with your friends! Later we'll sit around the campfire and talk about our day.

H Games day

Do you enjoy quizzes? Do you want to win super prizes – for example, a big bottle of soda, a box of chocolates, or a jar of candy? Play games in our new indoor community center with space for 200 people. A fun afternoon for everybody!

Reading: ______ /10

LISTEN

2 (55) **You'll hear a restaurant owner talking to some guests at a restaurant. Listen and write the missing information.**

Type of restaurant:	(1) ....
Owner's opinions:	Important to know where food comes from
	Bad for the (2) .... to transport food a long way
Lunch menu	Soup
	Pancakes with vegetables in a cream sauce with (3) .... (or rice)
	OR
	Omelette with onions, tomatoes, and spices with a bowl of salad and bread
	(If you're (4) .... anything, they can make something different)
Drinks	Apple juice from restaurant's own apples
	Milkshakes
Price of lunch menu	(5) $............

Listening: ______ /10

TEST-TAKING TIPS

listen and complete notes

- Read the information carefully before you listen.
- Decide what kind of information is missing.
- Listen for the words before the missing information.
- Write the exact words that you hear.

WRITE

3 Write a story (80–100 words) with the following first sentence:
I was eating dinner with my parents when something strange happened.

Writing: ______ /10

TEST-TAKING TIPS

write a story

- Read the task carefully.
- Think of the main events in your story and make notes.
- Use the simple past and past progressive to tell your story.
- Use time expressions to order the events in your story.
- Check the number of words.

Progress check score ______ /30

UNIT 5

WHO AM I?

IN THE PICTURE Different people

Talk about somebody's personality

ELENA (cheerful)

LINDA (sensitive)

WORK WITH WORDS

1 RECALL **Work in pairs. Match the speech bubbles to the correct personality adjectives in the box. You have three minutes.**

calm confident friendly funny ~~polite~~ rude serious shy

1 *Yes, please ... thank you.* polite

2 *Everything is OK.* ....

3 *Hello! How are you? I'm Jacob.* ....

4 *Ha! Ha! Do you know the joke about ... ?* ....

5 *I know I can do it if I really try!* ....

6 *I don't like big parties or speaking in front of the class.* ....

7 *I want pizza NOW!* ....

8 *You know, homework is very important.* ....

2 56 **Look at the pictures. Listen to the questions and say the correct names.**

3 57 **Listen and write the correct adjective from Exercise 2 for each description.**

1 *kind*

4 **What are they like? Complete the sentences with the correct adjectives from Exercise 2.**

1 Maria is very *cheerful*. She's always happy and positive.
2 I try to be .... when I go to the dentist, but I'm always scared!
3 Robert is really .... He shares everything.
4 I don't like playing tennis with Josh because he's so .... He hates losing.
5 Wanda is very .... She wants to be a model and study to be a doctor.
6 I'm very .... I cry at good and bad news!

5 **Write a short description of your personality. Use adjectives from Exercises 1 and 2. Give reasons if you can.**

I think I'm patient because I don't get angry when I wait. I'm usually cheerful but not in the morning. I hate getting up early!

6 **THE MOVING PICTURE** 58 **Watch the video. Match each person you meet in the video to the picture showing the same personality adjective. Who would you choose for a friend?**

SPEAK

7 **Work in pairs. Choose one person in the pictures. YOU are that person. Invent a profile for yourself. Take turns talking about your profile. Start like this:** *My name's … I'm … years old. I'm …*

How old are you?

What are you like?

What is your family like?

What do you like or not like?

MOVE BEYOND

Do the Words & Beyond exercise on page 73.

Workbook, page 132

READING Doodles and me

»» Identify the goal of a text

SPEAK AND READ

1 Look at the doodles on this page.

- Take a piece of paper and draw your own doodle.
- Show your doodle to a partner. Ask what your partner thinks it means.
- Do you agree? Why or why not?

PHRASE BYTES

That's good / pretty / funny!

It means you're creative / shy.

What is it?

2 a Read the tips in the HOW TO box.

b 59 Read the text and complete the sentence.

The goal of the text is to …

A give practical information (e.g., train times or opening times).

B explain how something works or what something means.

C tell people an opinion about something.

HOW TO

identify the goal of a text

- ☐ Look at the layout: Are there photos / diagrams / numbers? Is it a story / report / brochure?
- ☐ Read the title and the headings.
- ☐ Read the first lines of each part of the text.

What do your doodles say about you?

We doodle when we're bored with doing something or when we're waiting. Doodles can be shapes and patterns or objects. Some people believe your doodles (like handwriting or dreams) say something about your personality and feelings. So what do your doodles mean? Find out here!

Size and color

- Big doodles show you're confident. Small doodles show you're shy or want a quiet life.
- Dark colors mean you're serious, but bright colors mean you're feeling cheerful.

Shapes and patterns

- Triangles and squares or boxes mean you're organized and good at planning. Emotional people often draw circles and round shapes, while competitive people draw chess boards and other "game" shapes.
- Stars and arrows mean you're ambitious and you work hard.
- If you draw the same pattern many times, you're patient and good at concentrating.

Objects

- A nice face shows you're a cheerful and open person, but an ugly face means you're scared of trusting people. A funny face means you like attention.
- Kind, friendly people often draw flowers. Hearts mean you're in love – or want to be in love! Houses mean you want to be safe.
- All kinds of transportation mean you want to travel or get away from a problem. Butterflies and birds show you like being free and aren't interested in doing difficult tasks.
- Finally, if you often doodle your name, it shows you think about yourself a lot. The name of somebody else means you're thinking of that person.

3 Which tips in the HOW TO box did you use for help with Exercise 2b? Check (✓) them.

4 Read the text again and write the correct meaning(s).

1 small doodles *You're shy or want a quiet life.*
2 dark colors ______
3 circles ______
4 arrows ______
5 an ugly face ______
6 flowers ______
7 butterflies ______
8 your name ______

REACT

5 Work in pairs. What do you think? Tell your partner.

1 Do you agree with the explanation for your doodle from Exercise 1?
2 Do doodles and handwriting really say something about people? Why or why not?

Workbook, page 133

GRAMMAR Adjectives with prepositions + *-ing* form

5

Express your feelings about doing things

READ AND LISTEN Grammar in context

1 60 **Read and listen to the conversation. What is Diego good at? What was he scared of? Why?**

Reporter:	How did you become **interested in making** your own comic books?
Diego:	Well, I'm **not bad at telling** stories, and I was always **good at drawing** and **good at art**. But I was **bored with drawing** plants and things in art class at school. And I was **tired of reading** bad comic books!
Reporter:	Your parents must be proud of you.
Diego:	Well, I was really **scared of showing** them my first comic book. I was **worried about hearing** their opinion. But they loved it! Now I have a website. I'm really **excited about showing** other people my work.

STUDY

2 Complete the table. Use Exercise 1 to help you.

Adjectives followed by prepositions

Adjective	Preposition
bad / not so good	*at*
bored	....
excited	....
good / not bad	....
interested	....
scared	....
tired	....
worried	....

3 Complete the examples from Exercise 1.

Adjectives followed by prepositions and nouns

Expressions with prepositions are followed by a noun. A gerund is a noun formed from a verb. It ends with *-ing*.

adjective + preposition + noun
I was always good at ....

Adjective + preposition + gerund
I was always good at ....

Find more examples of adjective + preposition in Exercise 1.

See GRAMMAR DATABASE, page 68.

Workbook, pages 134–135

PRACTICE

4 Complete Rachel's sentences. Use the correct prepositions from Exercise 2 and the *-ing* form of the verbs.

I'm really excited (1) *about taking* (take) a digital art class this summer. I was always interested (2) .... (take) photos. Then I got some photo software. I was a litte worried (3) .... (use) it – it looked hard! But now I'm really good (4) .... (create) things with it. I never get bored (5) .... (change) photos on my computer, and I'm not scared (6) .... (try) new things.

5 Now write sentences for these students. Use the phrases in Exercise 2 and the *-ing* form of the verbs in the box.

cook dance ~~paint~~ run sing ski

1 "I'm *good at / not bad at painting*."
2 "I'm ...."
3 "I'm ...."
4 "I'm ...."
5 "I'm ...."
6 "I'm ...."

SPEAK

6 Work in pairs. Think about your answers to these questions. Then ask and answer.

1 What are you good (or not bad) at doing?
2 What are you bad (or not so good) at doing?
3 What are you interested in doing?
4 What are you tired of doing?
5 What are you scared of doing?
6 What are you excited about doing in the future?

MOVE BEYOND

Write the answers to the questions in Exercise 6.

LISTENING AND VOCABULARY Where do I belong?

Recognize when speakers need time to think

SPEAK AND LISTEN

PHRASE BYTES

My parents are from …
I was born in …
I speak … (and …)

1 **Work in pairs. Answer the questions.**

1 Where are your parents from?
2 Where were you born?
3 What language(s) do you speak?

2 **61 Listen to some students at an international school in Mexico. Match the students to the countries of their parents and the languages the students speak.**

Arabic
Brazil
Egypt
English
France
French
Portuguese
Mexico
Spanish
USA
Japan
Japanese

HOW TO

recognize when speakers need time to think

☐ Listen for words and sounds with no real meaning: *um, uh, ah, well, you know, like.*

☐ Listen carefully to the information after these sounds and words.

3 a **Read the tips in the HOW TO box.**

b **61 Listen again and choose the correct answer.**

1 English is Joshua's easiest language because …
A he speaks it at school.
(B) he speaks it at home.
C the grammar is easy.

2 When she graduates from high school, Amelie …
A is going to go to college.
B is going to travel.
C doesn't know what she wants to do.

3 Hiro feels he belongs in Mexico because …
A he speaks the language.
B his family lives there.
C he was born there.

4 **Which tips in the HOW TO box did you use for help with Exercise 3b? Check (✓) them.**

REACT

5 **Work in pairs. Order the things on the list from 1–5 (1 = most important). Then compare with your partner.**

What makes you belong to a place?
where you were born ☐
where you speak the language ☐
where your family is ☐
where your friends are ☐
where you like the weather, food, and people ☐

WORK WITH WORDS

6 **62 Work in pairs. Make a table. Write the nationality and language for each country in the box. Listen and check. In which three countries is the language not the same as the nationality?**

Brazil China Egypt
France Germany
USA Japan

Arabic Chinese English
French Portuguese German
Japanese

Country	Nationality	Language
Brazil	*Brazilian*	

7 **63 PRONOUNCE Listen to the words in your table in Exercise 6. Underline the stress. Then listen again and repeat the words.**

8 **Work in pairs. Student A looks at page 75. Student B looks at page 76. Ask and answer the quiz questions. Who can answer the most?**

MOVE BEYOND

Do the Words & Beyond exercise on page 73.

Workbook, pages 136–137

GRAMMAR Hopes, plans, and predictions

Talk about your hopes and plans, and predict events in the future

READ AND LISTEN

Grammar in context

1 64 **Fernanda lives in the USA, but her parents come from Peru. Read and listen to the interview. Where does she think she'll live in the future? Why?**

Interviewer: What are you going to do when you graduate from school? (1) ____

Fernanda: I'm definitely going to do something with music. (2) ____ I might be a singer. Or I may be a music teacher. (3) ____

Interviewer: Do you think you'll live in the USA or Peru in the future? (4) ____

Fernanda: I probably won't live in Peru. (5) ____ I hope I'll go there on vacation a lot. (6) ____ But my parents are going to stay in the USA. (7) ____ So I'll probably stay here too. (8) ____

STUDY

2 a Look at the interview again. Write *hope*, *plan*, or *prediction* for each sentence (1–8).

b Choose the correct options.

Hopes, plans, and predictions for the future

For plans, use ***will* / *be going to***.
For predictions, use ***will* / *be going to***.
For hopes, use *hope* + ***will* / *be going to***.

subject + *be* + going to + verb
I ***am*** */* ***is*** */* ***are*** *going to do something with music.*
She ***am*** */* ***is*** */* ***are*** *going to live in Peru.*
My parents ***am*** */* ***is*** */* ***are*** *going to stay in the USA.*

See GRAMMAR DATABASE, page 68.

3 Underline *definitely*, *probably*, *may*, and *might* in Exercise 1. Then choose the correct options.

Degrees of certainty

definitely = ***100 percent*** / ***75 percent*** sure
probably = ***100 percent*** / ***75 percent*** sure
may/might = ***100 percent*** / ***50 percent*** sure

Word order
I'll probably …
I probably won't …

See GRAMMAR DATABASE, page 68.

PRACTICE

4 a Read Alex's sentences about his future. Choose the correct options.

1 This evening I want to do my homework. I*'m not going to watch* / *won't watch* TV.
2 This weekend I'm doing the rest of my homework. I *may finish* / *'m going to finish* my project for Monday.
3 When I graduate from school, I hope I *'ll get* / *might get* a good job and a nice apartment.
4 I *may live* / *'ll live* in a different country, but I really don't know.
5 I think hard work is important. I *'ll definitely work* / *may work* a lot.
6 I plan to have a long life. I *won't be* / *'ll probably be* alive when I'm a hundred!

b Read Alex's sentences again. What adjective describes his personality?

5 Put the words in order to make questions. Then write your answers.

1 you / going to do / this evening / are / What / ?
What are you going to do this evening?
____
2 are / What / on the weekend / you / going to do / ?
____
3 you'll do / What / when you graduate from school / do you hope / ?
____
4 live / in the future / Where / you / might / ?
____
5 you / What other things / probably do / will / ?
____
6 won't / probably do / you / What / ?
____

SPEAK

6 Work in pairs.

- Choose a "personality" from the box. (Don't tell your partner!)
- Ask and answer the questions in Exercise 5. Your answers should match your personality.
- Guess your partner's personality.

brave cheerful
competitive
creative kind
lazy sensitive
shy smart

Workbook, page 138

LANGUAGE & BEYOND

THINGS I'm good at

making lists S
remembering song lyrics
helping my friends with their homework
watching TV
spelling
playing the piano
being patient with my little sister
running
taking photos
making other people laugh
singing in the shower
fixing the car with my dad
brushing my teeth
finding information on the internet
baking cookies
being on time
keeping my room clean
speaking English
sleeping

››› Recognize what you're good at

KNOW YOURSELF

READ

1 **Read Patrick's list above. Which do you think is his most important skill? Tell the class.**

2 **Look at the list again. Write the letters next to the skills. Some skills can have more than one letter.**

Skill important for ...

- school and learning. (*S*)
- getting a future job. (*J*)
- relaxing / taking care of your health. (*R*)
- being a friend and getting along with people. (*P*)
- helping your family / home skills. (*F*)
- using technology. (*T*)

DO

3 **Make a list of things you're good at. Write as many things as possible.**

4 **Work in pairs. Exchange lists. Read your partner's list and put his or her skills in the categories in Exercise 2. Is your partner stronger in one category? Tell him or her.**

5 **Add at least three more things to his or her list. Pass the list back to your partner. Do you both agree?**

REFLECT

6 **Discuss the questions with your class. Do you agree with the REFLECTION POINT?**

1 How often do you worry about things you're bad at or you can't do?
2 How or when do you use your skills?
3 How often do you tell other people they're good at something?

REFLECTION POINT

Think about all the things you're good at – not the things you're bad at.

Use your skills!

Tell other people when they're good at things.

EXTEND

7 **Work in a group. Plan a group "Real Talent Show."**

- Write one thing each person in your group can do. (It can be something amazing, an everyday skill, or something silly.)
- Present your program for the show to the class.
- Which act would you most like to see?

››› Workbook, page 141

SPEAKING Can I help?

Offer help and express spontaneous decisions

SPEAK

1 Work in pairs. Look at the photos. What are the people in the photos doing?

PHRASE BYTES

He's / She's listening to / looking at …

Maybe …

LISTEN

2 65 Listen to the conversations. What problems do Sam and Lynn have?

1

Karina: What's wrong?
Sam: I downloaded this great song, but the lyrics are in Spanish. You know I don't speak Spanish.
Karina: But I understand Spanish. (1) __________ to the song and translate it?
Sam: That would be great, thanks. You're so smart!
Karina: No problem.

2

Al: What's wrong?
Lynn: I'm trying to learn these lines for the school play. I can't remember them.
Al: Don't worry, (2) __________ you. (3) __________ the lines with you. (4) __________ over to your house later.
Lynn: Thanks! That's really generous of you.

3 65 How are Karina and Al going to help? Complete the conversations with the expressions in the box. Then listen again and check.

I can practice | I'll come | I'll help | Would you like me to listen

ACT

4 Read the situations below. Work in pairs. One person explains his or her problem. The other offers help. Use the conversations to help you.

- you can't do your physics homework
- you aren't very good at computer games and don't understand a game
- you can't find a room at school
- you're worried about wearing the wrong thing for a party

PHRASEBOOK 66

Offer help / Make a spontaneous decision

Would you like me to listen / do … ?

I'll help you / explain …

I can practice / translate …

React

Thanks.

That would be great, thanks.

Workbook, page 63

WRITING Time capsule

Use *because* and *so*

SPEAK AND READ

1 **Tell the class your thoughts about the future. Choose A, B, or C, or complete D.**

A I never think about the future. I have a great life now.
B I think about the future a lot. I have a lot of exciting plans!
C I worry about the future a lot.
D I …

2 **a** **Read the tips in the HOW TO box.**

b **Read Adele's predictions for the time capsule. Answer the questions.**

1 What does she hope will happen in three years?
2 What does she predict will happen in three years?

HOW TO

use *because* and *so*

- Use *because* before a reason (to explain why).

  Adele has a lot of friends ***because*** *she's kind and generous.*

- Use so before a result (what happens next).

  Adele is kind and generous, ***so*** *she has a lot of friends.*

  Note: Use a comma before so.

Time Capsule - Open in three years

I'll probably get another dog because I love dogs so much. I won't get tired of taking care of dogs.

I'm good at science and I'm interested in doing experiments, so I might study biology in high school.

I hope I'll improve in math because I need math for my science class.

I hope I'll still be best friends with Emilia, Gina, and Lucia.

I'm very good at drawing and I'm going to start painting, so I'll probably continue taking art.

Adele

PRACTICE

3 **Complete the sentences with *because* or *so*.**

1 I hope to go to Italy on vacation *because* I love pasta.
2 I'm going to train hard ________ I want to be on the team.
3 I'm going to go to bed earlier ________ I'm not always tired.
4 I'd like to learn Japanese ________ I can read Japanese comic books.
5 I'm going to study hard ________ I want to get good grades.

DISCUSS

4 **Talk about events you think will happen to you in three years.**

WRITE

5 **Write predictions about yourself. Imagine that you'll put this information in a time capsule and open it in three years.**

1 Write five predictions and hopes. Use *hope, will probably,* and *might*. Think about your school, your friends, and your hobbies. Predict what will happen in three years.

2 Explain why you think your predictions will come true. Use *because* and so to connect your ideas. Use *because* with a reason. Use *so* with a result. See the HOW TO box.

3 Use adjectives followed by prepositions to describe yourself and your interests.

SHARE

6 **Make a list of predictions and hopes that are similar for everyone in your class.**

Workbook, pages 140–141

The Student Space: the place to meet interesting students from all over the world!

home | who we are! | what we do | forum | about us | sign in | register

VOCABULARY Personality adjectives

1 Complete the personality adjectives.

You can meet different kinds of people!

I'm very (1) c______ and I like to win.
I'm also very (2) a______ and want to be successful.
I'm very (3) b______ too – I'm never scared.
I'm very (4) c______. I don't worry about things.

I'm very (5) s______ and good at math and puzzles.
I'm very (6) p______ and can wait for things.
I'm very (7) g______ and share (nearly) everything.

I'm very (8) c______ and have a lot of ideas.
I'm very (9) k______ and help people.
I'm very (10) s______ and cry a lot.

___ /10

Countries, nationalities, and languages

2 Write the correct nationalities or languages.

Make friends from all over the world.

Fleur: My parents are from France and Egypt, and we live in Italy.
I speak (1) ______, (2) ______, and (3) ______.

Tomás: I'm from Colombia, but we lived in China and Vietnam when I was small. I speak (4) ______, (5) ______, and (6) ______.

Karin: I was born in Japan, but my parents are from Russia and Germany.
I speak (7) ______, (8) ______, and (9) ______.

Paul: We live in Argentina, but my dad is from Brazil and my mom is from the USA.
I speak (10) ______, (11) ______, and (12) ______.

___ /12

GRAMMAR Adjectives with prepositions + *-ing* form

3 Choose the correct options and write the *-ing* form of the verbs.

Find people like you.

PAUL

1 I'm scared *of* / *at* ______ to girls. (talk)
2 I'm good *in* / *at* ______ jokes. (tell)
3 I'm worried *with* / *about* ______ the test. (take)
4 I'm bored *with* / *in* ______ TV. (watch)
5 I'm excited *of* / *about* ______ to the party. (go)
6 I'm interested *in* / *at* ______ the guitar. (play)

___ /12

Hopes, plans, and predictions

4 Complete the interview with *going to*, *'ll*, *won't*, or *might*.

Talk about your dreams for the future.

KARIN

I plan to enjoy my life! I'm (1) ______ have fun. I'm not (2) ______ worry about things. I think I (3) ______ have a creative job. I (4) ______ be a painter … or a writer … or a dancer … (I don't really know). I plan to travel. I'm (5) ______ see the world. I (6) ______ probably live in different places. I probably (7) ______ have much money. I just hope I (8) ______ be happy!

___ /16

Your score: ___ /50

SKILLS CHECK

✓✓✓ Yes, I can. No problem!
✓✓ Yes, I can. But I need a little help.
✓ Yes, I can. But I need a lot of help.

I can identify the goal of a text. ______
I can recognize when speakers need time to think. ______
I can recognize what I'm good at. ______
I can offer help and express spontaneous decisions. ______
I can use *because* and *so* when I write. ______

Workbook, pages 142–143

READ

1 **Read the text and choose the correct word (A, B, C, or D) for each blank.**

Science and Art

Museums are fantastic places for (1) __________ about art and science.

In science museums, you can find out about scientists and inventors, and other topics you (2) __________ be interested in. You can learn about the history of machines and other forms of technology. Science museums are also great (3) __________ you get to see a lot of unique inventions and sometimes even interact with some of them.

Are you (4) __________ art? In art galleries, you will see amazing sculptures, paintings, drawings, and many other forms of art. You can (5) __________ learn a lot about the lives of the artists who created the artwork as well.

If you haven't been to a museum before, be sure to check one out when you get a chance. You will be glad you did.

	A	B	C	D
1	A going	B learning	C doing	D studying
2	A am	B will	C won't	D might
3	A because	B so	C probably	D for
4	A going to	B worried about	C scared of	D interested in
5	A so	B probably	C hope	D might

Reading: ______ /10

TEST-TAKING TIPS

complete a multiple-choice text with blanks

- Quickly read the text. What's it about? What's its goal?
- Read it again. Think what the word for each blank might be.
- Look at the choices. Is your word there?
- If not, look at the other choices. Which word fits best?

LISTEN

2 ▶67 **You'll hear a school career counselor talking to a class. Check (✓) the correct box for each question.**

1 The students need to decide …
A what job they want to do. ☐
B what new subjects to study next year. ☐
C whether to study math and science next year. ☐

2 Maggie advises the students to …
A think about what they're good and bad at. ☐
B study a new language. ☐
C only study drama if they're confident. ☐

3 To help them make the right decision, students …
A can ask Maggie questions. ☐
B can invite other people to their class. ☐
C will hear other teachers talking about their subjects. ☐

4 When they talk to their parents, Maggie says students should …
A only talk about serious subjects. ☐
B tell them what they really want to study. ☐
C ask their parents to make decisions. ☐

5 The students have to …
A take a form home so that their parents can sign it. ☐
B read a form and then sign it. ☐
C read a form when they get home. ☐

Listening: ______ /10

TEST-TAKING TIPS

answer multiple-choice questions

- Read the instructions. What are you going to hear?
- Read the questions and choices. Underline important words.
- Listen. Decide which choices aren't possible.
- Listen again. Choose the best of the possible options.

WRITE

3 Complete the second sentence so that it means the same as the first. Use no more than three words.

1 I'm a good language learner.
I'm good ______ languages.
2 Her plan is to study art next year.
She's ______ art next year.
3 He might go to Peru on vacation.
He will ______ vacation in Peru.
4 What will you do when you graduate from school?
What are you ______ when you graduate from school?

______ /4

4 Some American students visiting your school want to meet you and your friends this weekend. Write them a message (35–45 words).

- Say what plans you have on Saturday.
- Mention other possible plans and how they depend on the weather.
- Say why you can't meet on Sunday.

______ /6

Writing: ______ /10

TEST-TAKING TIPS

write a message

- Read the task carefully. Who are you writing to?
- Plan your message before you write.
- Include phrases to start and end your message.
- Use *because* before a reason and *so* before a result.

Progress check score ______ /30

Simple present

USE

Use the simple present to talk about

- habits and routines:
  I ***use*** *my cell phone to check my mail.*
  I ***don't*** *often* ***play*** *video games.*
- things that are generally true:
  The brain ***uses*** *a lot of energy in the day.*

FORM

Affirmative

- The simple present for *I*, *you*, *we*, and *they* is the same. For the *he/she/it* forms, add -s, -es, or -ies to the verb.

I/You/We/They	**watch**	TV.
He/She/It	**chats**	online.

Spelling: *he/she/it* forms

- If a verb ends in -o, add -es:
  Ana ***goes*** *to the computer club at school.*
- If a verb ends in a consonant and -y, change the -y to -i and add -es:
  Dylan always ***tries*** *to do his homework before dinner.*
- If a verb ends in -s, -z, -x, -ch, or -sh, add -es:
  He ***teaches*** *French at my school.*

Negative

- Form the simple present negative with *don't (do not)* or *doesn't (does not)* + verb.

I/You/We/They	**don't**	**log on**	every day.
He/She/It	**doesn't**	**send**	emails.

- In informal speech and writing, you usually use the contractions *don't* and *doesn't.*

WATCH OUT! In negative sentences, don't add -s to the verb after *doesn't*:
He doesn't ***speak*** *French.* (not ~~*He doesn't speaks French.*~~)

Questions and short answers

- Form questions in the simple present with *do/does* + subject + verb.

Do	I/you/we/they	**speak** English?
Does	he/she/it	**go** on the internet?

Yes,	I/you/we/they	**do.**
	he/she/it	**does.**
No,	I/you/we/they	**don't.**
	he/she/it	**doesn't.**

Question words

- To ask questions in the simple present, use question word + *do/does* + subject + verb:
  What *do you think about the video?*

Adverbs and expressions of frequency

USE

- Use adverbs and expressions of frequency to say how often you do something:
  My dad ***never*** *logs on during the week.*
  I log on ***every night.***
- The main **adverbs** of frequency are (in order of frequency):

0% *never*
hardly ever / rarely
sometimes/occasionally
often/regularly
usually/normally
100% *always*

- Adverbs of frequency usually go before the main verb and after *be*, *can*, and *do/does*:
  I'm ***always*** *logged on.*
  He ***doesn't often play*** *video games.*
- The main expressions of frequency are (in order of frequency):
  occasionally / from time to time / now and then / every evening/day/week
- Expressions of frequency go at the beginning or end of a sentence:
  We go on vacation ***once or twice a year.***

Articles: *a/an*, *the* and zero article

a/an

Use (a/an)

- before one example of a thing:
  I have ***a new tablet.***
- before somebody's job:
  My sister is ***a teacher.***
- Use *an* when the noun begins with a vowel:
  My phone has ***an app*** *for history homework.*

the

Use *the* before:

- a specific thing:
  He bought ***the green cell phone.***
- something there is only one of:
  The internet *is very useful for homework.*
- superlatives and dates:
  The Cornerhouse is ***the best café*** *in the city.*
  My birthday is on ***the 21st of June.***
- something already mentioned:
  There's a computer club at my school. ***The club*** *is on Thursday.*
- countries and places with a plural name:
  I'm going on vacation to ***the United States.***

zero article

Don't use an article before:

- plural or uncountable nouns:
  Many teenagers like playing ***video games.***
  We get math ***homework*** *every day.*
- things in general:
  It's useful to have ***maps*** *on a cell phone.*
- meals, days, streets, singular place names:
  I eat ***lunch*** *in the cafeteria.*
  He lives in ***Chicago.***

Present progressive review

USE

- Use the present progressive to talk about things in progress now or around now:
  *Josh is busy. He's **cooking** dinner.*
  *It **isn't raining** now. Let's go out.*
  *What **are** you **doing**?*
  ***Are** you **studying** for the math test?*

Present progressive and simple present

- Use the present progressive to talk about things in progress now or around now, and the simple present for habits and routines and things that are generally true:
  *We **usually have** pizza on Fridays, but today **we're having** pasta.*
- Use time expressions such as *now, right now,* or *today* with the present progressive:
  ***I'm studying** for my math test **right now**.*
- Use time expressions such as *on Wednesdays, every week, never, usually*, and *always* with the simple present:
  *I **always do** the dishes after dinner.*

FORM

Affirmative

- Form the present progressive with *be* + *-ing* form of the verb.

I'm	reading	a book.
You're		
He's/She's		
It's	raining.	
We're	watching	TV.
They're		

Spelling

- If a verb ends in *-e*, remove the final *-e* before adding *-ing*:
  take – taking *use – using*
- If a verb ends in a vowel (e.g., *i, a, o*) and a consonant (e.g., *m, p, t*), double the consonant before adding *-ing:*
  swim – swimming *shop – shopping*
- If a verb ends in *-ie*, change the *-ie* to *-y* before adding *-ing*:
  lie – lying

Negative

- Form the present progressive negative with *be* + *not* + *-ing* form of the verb.

I'm not	doing	the laundry.
You aren't		
He/She isn't		
It isn't	working.	
We/They aren't	cooking	dinner.

- You usually use the contractions of *be* in the present progressive:
  *He's **waiting** for the bus.*

Questions and short answers

- Form present progressive questions with *be* + subject + *-ing* form of the verb.

Am	I	**making** a lot of noise?	Yes, you are. / No, you aren't.
Are	you	**coming** tonight?	Yes, I am. / No, I'm not.
Is	he/she		Yes, he/she is. / No, he/she isn't.
	it	**snowing**	Yes, it is. / No, it isn't.
Are	we/they	**being** silly?	Yes, we/they are. / No, we/they aren't.

- You can also use question words (*What, Who, Where, How*) before *be*:
  ***Where are** you **staying** in Miami?*

WATCH OUT! You never use contractions in affirmative short answers:
*Yes, **I am.*** (not ~~*Yes, I'm.*~~)

Stative verbs

- You don't usually use the present progressive with stative verbs like *like, know, need, understand*, and *want*. Use the simple present:
  *Nasrin really **likes** that book.* (not ~~*Nasrin is really liking that book.*~~)
  *I **don't understand** the question.* (not ~~*I'm not understanding the question.*~~)
- Other stative verbs are:
  agree, believe, hate, love, remember

WATCH OUT! You don't usually use the present progressive with *hear*, *see*, or *smell*. Use *can/can't* instead:
*I **can't hear** you. Can you say that again?*
(not ~~*I'm not hearing you*~~ …)

Present progressive for future arrangements

USE

- Use the present progressive to talk about arrangements at specific times in the future:
  ***I'm cooking** dinner this evening.*
  *Dad's **taking** me to the soccer game on Saturday.*
  *We **aren't going** anywhere this weekend.*
  *What **are** you **doing** tomorrow night?*
- These are often travel plans or arrangements with other people:
  ***We're meeting Mario and Alyssa** downtown this afternoon.*
- You often use time expressions with the present progressive for future arrangements, such as:

tomorrow on the/this weekend
this evening/afternoon tonight
on Monday/Tuesday at seven o'clock
next week/month/year in the summer
in two weeks at the end of the month

Simple past

USE

Use the simple past to talk about:

- completed actions in the past:
  Two months later Felix ***planted*** *his first tree.*
- actions that happened at a specific time in the past:
  In 2004, Wangari Maathai ***won*** *the Nobel Peace Prize.*
- You often use these time phrases with the simple past:

yesterday   yesterday morning/afternoon   last night/week
an hour/two months ago   on Monday   in July/2011

FORM

Affirmative

Regular verbs

- Form the simple past of regular verbs with verb + *-ed*.

I/You/He/She/It/We/They	**started**	middle school in 2013.

Spelling

- If a verb ends in *-y*, change the *y* to *i* and add *-ed*:
  *study – stud**ied***
  But not if there's a vowel before the *-y*:
  *play – play**ed***
- If a verb ends in a vowel (e.g., *o*) and a consonant (e.g., *p*, *t*), double the consonant before adding *-ed*:
  *stop – sto**pped***

Irregular verbs

- Many verbs are irregular in the simple past. You have to learn these: *give* – ***gave***, *say* – ***said***, *see* – ***saw***, *make* – ***made***. (*See page 140 for a list of irregular verbs in the simple past.*)

Negative

- Form the negative simple past with *didn't* (*did not*) + verb.

I/You/He/She/It/We/They	**didn't look**	nervous.

- Use the contraction *didn't* in informal speech and writing.

Questions and short answers

- Form simple past questions with *Did* + subject + verb.

Did	you/he/she/it/we/they	**win** a prize?
Yes,	I/you/he/she/it/we/they	**did**.
No,	I/you/he/she/it/we/they	**didn't**.

- You can also use question words *What, Who, Where, How* before *did*: ***Where did*** *you* ***go*** *last night?*

Past progressive

USE

Use the past progressive to:

- talk about actions in progress in the past:
  While we ***were swimming*** *in the ocean, we saw a dolphin.*
- talk about something happening at a particular time in the past:
  At six o'clock last night I ***was doing*** *my homework.*
- describe background events, often to set the scene in a story: *It* ***was raining****. He* ***was walking*** *slowly along the beach when he suddenly saw a large creature.*

FORM

Affirmative

- Past form of *be* + *-ing* form of the verb.

I/He/She/It	**was**	**walking**.
You/We/They	**were**	**talking**.

Negative

- Wasn't *(was not)* or *weren't (were not)* + *-ing* form of the verb.

I/He/She/It	**wasn't**	**moving**.
You/We/They	**weren't**	**sleeping**.

- You usually use the contractions *wasn't* and *weren't* in informal speech and writing.

Questions and short answers

- Form questions in the past progressive with *was/were* + subject + *-ing* form of verb.

Were	you/we/they	**talking**?	Yes, you/we/they **were**. No, you/we/they **weren't**.
Was	I/he/she/it	**watching** the owl?	Yes, I/he/she/it **was**. No, I/he/she/it **wasn't**.

Past progressive and simple past

- Use the past progressive for actions in progress and the simple past for completed actions:
  One day we ***were walking*** *near a river* ***when*** *I* ***saw*** *a snake.*
- Use *while* before the past progressive and *when* before the simple past:
  Was it raining when you were out? No, it wasn't.
  Were they watching TV yesterday afternoon? Yes, they were.

- You can also use question words *What, Who, Where, How,* before *was/were*:
  What were *you* ***doing*** *yesterday at ten o'clock?*

WATCH OUT! Some verbs change their spelling in the *-ing* form.
See Grammar Database 2 on page 121 for more information.

- Don't use the past progressive with stative verbs, or *hear*, *see*, or *smell*:
  We ***didn't understand*** *him.* (not ~~*We weren't understanding him.*~~)
  See Grammar Database 2 on page 121 for more information.

Countable and uncountable

Countable nouns

- are nouns you can count:
  eggs, onions, lemons
- use *a/an* or *the* in the singular:
  *Beat **an egg**.* *Chop **the onion**.*
- use *some, a few, many, a lot of*, or a number with the plural:
  ***Many recipes** from Italy use cheese.*
- have a singular and a plural form:
  the onion *the onions*
- take a singular or plural verb:
  *A lot of **diets don't work**.*
  ***The chef gave** some good tips on how to make omelettes.*

Uncountable nouns

- don't use *a/an* or a number with them but you can use *the*:
  *Put **the cheese** on the pancake.*
- often use *some, a lot, a little*:
  ***Some** oil is added.*
- usually take a singular verb:
  *A little dark **chocolate** every day **is** good for you.*

Expressions of quantity

a lot of

- Use *a lot of* to describe a large quantity of something. You can use this with both countable and uncountable nouns:
  *There is **a lot of bread**.* *I have **a lot of friends**.*
- You can also use *many* but only with countable nouns:
  *There are **many good recipes** for pancakes.*
  You can use *many* in negative sentences and questions too.

a little / a few

- Use *a little* or *a few* to describe a small quantity of something.
- Use *a little* with uncountable nouns:
  *Add **a little milk** to the mixture.*
- Use *a few* with countable nouns:
  *I have **a few eggs** but not many.*

some

- Use *some* to describe an amount that is not big and not small. You can use *some* with countable and uncountable nouns:
  *There are **some vegetables** but not many.*
  *Heat **some oil** in a pan.*

Negative

- Use *any* in negative sentences to talk about zero amounts. You can use this with both countable and uncountable nouns:
  *There aren't **any onions**.* *I don't have **any bread**.*
- You can also use *no* with both countable and uncountable nouns:
  ***No onions** are needed for this dish.*
  *There's **no milk** in the refrigerator.*
- Use *not + many* with countable nouns and *not + much* with uncountable nouns to talk about a small amount of something in negative sentences:
  *I don't need **many eggs** to make an omelette.*
  *He doesn't have **much** time.*
- You can also use *not + a lot of* with both countable and uncountable nouns:
  *It **doesn't** have **a lot of spices** in it.*
  *I **didn't** have **a lot of help** with this dish.*

Questions

- Use *any* with countable and uncountable nouns to ask about quantity:
  *Do you have **any milk**?* *Are there **any eggs** in the refrigerator?*

Note: You can also use *some* when making requests or offers. You can use it with countable and uncountable nouns:
*Can I have **some ketchup** with the fries, please?*
*Would you like **some onions** with your burger?*

How much? / How many?

- You can use *How many* or *How much* to ask about quantity. Use *How many* for countable nouns and *How much* for uncountable nouns:
  ***How many eggs** do you need?*
  ***How much food** do supermarkets throw away?*

Short answers

- You can answer a *How many* or *How much* question with *none, a few/little, not much/many, a lot:*
  How much milk** do we have?* ***Not much.

Indefinite pronouns

USE

- Use indefinite pronouns to talk about people, things, or places that are not specific:
  *I have **something** small for lunch since I'm not usually hungry.*
  *After she'd made the cake, there was flour **everywhere**.*
  ***Nobody** wanted to help clean up.*
  *We aren't going **anywhere** this weekend.*

FORM

Affirmative sentences

People	Things	Places
somebody	something	somewhere
everybody	everything	everywhere
nobody	nothing	nowhere

- Use the ending *-body* with people.
- Use the ending *-thing* with objects.
- Use the ending *-where* with places.
- You can also use *-one* with people: *someone, everyone, no one:*
  ***No one** likes waste.* ***Someone** ate the last cookie!*

Negative sentences and questions

People	Things	Places
anybody/anyone	anything	anywhere

- Use *anybody/anyone, anything, anywhere* in negative sentences:
  *I **don't** know **anyone** who likes spinach.*
  *I **can't** find the recipe **anywhere**.*
- Use *anybody, anything, anywhere* in questions if you don't know if the thing, person, or place exists:
  *Is there **anything** to eat?*

WATCH OUT! Indefinite pronouns use a singular verb:
*Everyone **knows** the answer.*
(not ~~*Everyone know the answer.*~~)

Adjectives followed by prepositions and nouns

USE AND FORM

An adjective + preposition can be followed by a gerund. A gerund is a noun formed from a verb. It ends with *-ing*.

Use an adjective + preposition + gerund to describe

- how good someone is at doing something:
  *He's **good at painting**.*
  *Leah's **not bad at playing** the piano.*
- how someone feels about doing something:
  *She's **worried about talking** to the teacher.*
  *Pete was **tired of watching** movies.*

Spelling

- Remember that if a verb ends in *-e*, drop the final *-e* before adding *-ing*:
  take – taking   *use – using*

See Grammar Database 2 on page 121 for more information.

Which preposition?

Adjective	Preposition
tired/scared	of
(not so) good / (not) bad	at
excited/worried	about
bored	with
interested	in

Note: After *bored*, you can use *of* or *with*:
*He was **bored of/with** playing computer games.*

Note: An adjective + preposition can come before a noun:
*He's good at **art**.*

Hopes, plans, and predictions for the future

Future plans: *be* + *going to* + verb

USE

- Use *be* + *going to* + verb to talk about plans in the future (when you have already made a decision):
  ***I'm going to visit** my grandparents this summer.*
  ***What are you going to do** when you graduate from school?*

FORM

Affirmative

I'm	going to	study geography in college.
You're/We're/They're		
He's/She's/It's		

Negative

I'm **not**	going to	travel around the world.
You/We/They **aren't**		
He/She/It **isn't**		

Questions and short answers

- Form questions with *be* + subject + *going to* + verb.

Questions			Short answers
Am I	going to	go to college?	**Yes**, I **am**. / **No**, I'm **not**.
Is he/she/it	going to		**Yes**, he/she/it **is**. / **No**, he/she/it **isn't**.
Are you/we/they	going to		**Yes**, you/we/they **are**. / **No**, you/we/they **aren't**.

Degrees of certainty

USE

- Use *will / will not* + verb for predictions about the future:
  *I'll probably **see** a lot of different countries.*
- Use *hope* + *will / will not* + verb for hopes for the future:
  *She hopes she**'ll get** a good job.*
- Use *may* or *might* + verb if you are unsure if something will happen or not:
  *I **may go** to college.*   *He **might be** a dancer.*
- You can also use *I think* or *I don't think* with *will* if you're not sure:
  ***I think I'll study** to be an engineer.*
  ***I don't think I'll live** in another country.*
- Use *definitely* or *probably* to say how sure it is that something will happen. Put *definitely/probably* after *'ll* and before *won't*:
  *I'll **definitely** travel to different countries.*
  *I **probably won't** live in Mexico.*
- You can also use *definitely* with *going to*:
  *I'm **definitely going to do** something with music.*

How sure is it?

definitely = **100 percent** sure
probably = **75 percent** sure
may/might = **50 percent** sure

FORM

will

Affirmative

- There's just one form of the verb.

I'll/You'll/He'll/She'll/It'll/We'll/They'll	**get** a good job.

Negative

- There's just one form of the verb.

I/You/He/She/It/We/They **won't**	**go** to college.

Questions and short answers

Questions		Short answers
Will I/you/he/she/it/we/they	stay at home?	**Yes**, I/you/he/she/it/we/they **will**. / **No**, I/you/he/she/it/we/they **won't**.

***What** do you think you**'ll** do when you graduate from school?*
***Do** you think you**'ll** live in your home town?*
***What** do you think you **won't** do?*

WORDS & BEYOND

Page 8

RECALL

COMMUNICATION AND TECHNOLOGY – DEVICES

camera
cell phone
computer
game console
laptop
MP3 player
tablet

WORK WITH WORDS

TIP: Look for words that are similar in your language. Note if the meaning is the same or different, and note if the spelling is a little different.

TASK: Which RECALL words are similar in your language?

Pages 8 and 9

APPLICATIONS (APPS)

app store
calculator
calendar
compass
games
mail
maps
messages
notes
social networking
videos
web browser

MOVE BEYOND

Which things on the word list do you use? Put the things in order, starting with the one you use most.

Page 12

COMPUTER PARTS

headphones
keyboard
microphone
monitor
mouse
printer
screen
speaker
USB port
webcam

MOVE BEYOND

1. **Check (✔) the computer parts you can see on a computer at home or at school.**
2. **Can you name any other computer parts? Draw a picture of the part or parts and write the name under it.**

OTHER IMPORTANT WORDS

ad
appliance
blog (n & v)
brain
chat online
connect
device
energy
find out
go on the internet
icon
internet connection
invention
log in/on
relax
suburb
switch off
technology company
text message
write code

Page 18

RECALL

KINDS OF HOMES
apartment
house

ROOMS
bathroom
bedroom
closet
dining room
hall
kitchen
living room

FURNITURE
armchair
bed
bookshelf
cabinet
carpet
chair
desk
shelf
sofa
table

APPLIANCES
clock
dishwasher
kettle
lamp
refrigerator
stove
washing machine

OTHER
bathtub
curtains
door
floor
light
phone
picture
radio
shower
sink

WORK WITH WORDS

TIP: Practice your vocabulary when you go to different places. Say the words.

TASK: Look around you now and find words on the RECALL list. Can you see any other things?

Pages 18 and 19

HOUSEHOLD CHORES
clean the room
clear the table
do the ironing
do the laundry
load the dishwasher
make the bed
mop the floor
set the table
sort the recycling
take out the trash
vacuum
wash the dishes

MOVE BEYOND
Write your five least favorite household chores from the list.

1 ....
2 ....
3 ....
4 ....
5 ....

Page 22

FREE-TIME ACTIVITIES
go ice skating
go shopping
go to the movies
listen to music
meet friends
play soccer
play an instrument
read a book
ride a bike
watch television

MOVE BEYOND
Write your three favorite free-time activities.

1 ....
2 ....
3 ....

Add an extra free-time activity you know in English.

4 ....

OTHER IMPORTANT WORDS
advantage
argue
chore
disadvantage
fair (adj)
feed the fish
generation
go out (with)
meeting place
mess
organization
originally
relatives
remote (control)
soap opera
study (for a test)
take turns
train (v)

WORDS & BEYOND

Page 30

RECALL

NATURAL FEATURES

beach
forest
island
mountain
ocean
river

WORK WITH WORDS

TIP: Writing examples in your vocabulary notes can help you remember new words.

TASK: Write local or famous examples of the RECALL words.

Pages 30 and 31

LANDSCAPES AND NATURAL FEATURES

coast
countryside
desert
field
flower
forest
grass
hill
ice sheet
island
lake
savannah
stream

MOVE BEYOND

Think of where you are now. What is the closest example of the natural features on the list?

....

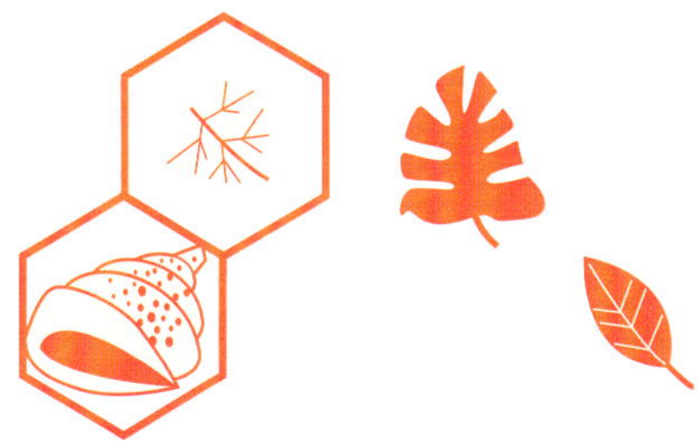

Page 34

WILDLIFE

LAND AND WATER ANIMALS	BIRDS	INSECTS	REPTILES
bear [ ]	owl [ ]	ant [ ]	crocodile [ ]
dolphin [ ]	parrot [ ]	bee [ ]	snake [ ]
frog [ ]	penguin [ ]	spider [ ]	turtle [ ]

MOVE BEYOND

Which wildlife on the list lives in your country? Check [✔] the right animals, birds, insects, and reptiles.

OTHER IMPORTANT WORDS

awake
bark (v)
campaign (n)
chase (v)
climate change
cover (v)
flashlight
go down
join
litter (n)
low
make a speech
plant (v)
reach a goal
save
scream (v)
sleeping bag
smell (v)
species
success
take part (in)
temperature

Page 40

RECALL

VEGETABLES	FRUIT	MEAT & FISH	DAIRY	OTHER	DRINKS
carrot	apple	chicken	butter	bread	coffee
onion	banana	steak	cheese	cake	juice
potato	grapes		ice cream	candy	mineral water
salad	lemon		milk	chocolate	soda
tomato	orange			egg	tea
				fries	
				oil	
				pasta	
				pizza	
				rice	
				sandwich	
				soup	

WORK WITH WORDS

TIP: Learn words in categories (e.g., vegetables, fruit).

TASK: Find words in RECALL for this category: sweet food and drinks.

Pages 40 and 41

KITCHEN EQUIPMENT

bowl
cutting board
frying pan
knife
saucepan

COOKING VERBS

beat
chop
cut
fry
heat
pour
stir

MOVE BEYOND

Complete the sentences with the correct equipment.

1 You cut something with a ....
2 You beat something in a ....
3 You cook something in a ....
4 You chop something on a ....
5 You fry something in a ....

Page 44

CONTAINERS AND AMOUNTS

bottle
box
can
carton
jar
loaf
package
piece

MOVE BEYOND

Complete the expressions with as many words as possible.

1 a package of ....
2 a bottle of ....
3 a carton of ....
4 a piece of ....

OTHER IMPORTANT WORDS

allergic (to something)
cookies
cream
delicious
dessert
diet (n)
flour
fresh
golden brown
jam
ketchup
lettuce
milkshake
omelette
pancake
pepper
salt
sauce
spices
throw away
vegetarian
waste (n & v)

WORDS & BEYOND

UNIT 5

Page 52

RECALL

PERSONALITY ADJECTIVES

calm	polite
cheerful	rude
friendly	serious
funny	shy

WORK WITH WORDS

TIP: Learn adjectives together with their opposites (e.g., *big* and *small*).

TASK: Find three pairs of opposites in the RECALL words.

Pages 52 and 53

PERSONALITY ADJECTIVES

ambitious
brave
competitive
confident
creative
sensitive
generous
kind
patient
smart

MOVE BEYOND

Write the name of a famous person (an athlete, politician, scientist, artist) for each personality adjective on the list.

Page 56

COUNTRY	NATIONALITY	LANGUAGE
Brazil	Brazilian	Portuguese
China	Chinese	Chinese
Egypt	Egyptian	Arabic
France	French	French
Germany	German	German
Haiti	Haitian	Creole
Italy	Italian	Italian
Japan	Japanese	Japanese
Mexico	Mexican	Spanish
Russia	Russian	Russian
Spain	Spanish	Spanish
USA	American	English
Vietnam	Vietnamese	Vietnamese

MOVE BEYOND

Write the countries from the list in …

… Africa.

… Asia.

… Central and South America.

… North America.

… Europe.

OTHER IMPORTANT WORDS

arrow	personality
belong	shape
circle (n)	square
doodle (n & v)	triangle
pattern (n & v)	trust (v)

Adjectives followed by prepositions

bad at	interested in
bored with	scared of
excited about	tired of
good at	worried about

IRREGULAR VERBS

base verb	simple past	past participle
be	was/were	been
beat	beat	beaten
become	became	become
begin	began	begun
blow	blew	blown
break	broke	broken
bring	brought	brought
build	built	built
buy	bought	bought
choose	chose	chosen
come	came	come
cost	cost	cost
cut	cut	cut
deal	dealt	dealt
do	did	done
draw	drew	drawn
drink	drank	drunk
drive	drove	driven
eat	ate	eaten
fall	fell	fallen
feed	fed	fed
feel	felt	felt
fight	fought	fought
find	found	found
fly	flew	flown
forget	forgot	forgotten
get	got	gotten
give	gave	given
go	went	gone
grow	grew	grown
hang (out)	hung (out)	hung (out)
have	had	had
hear	heard	heard
hit	hit	hit
hold	held	held
hurt	hurt	hurt
keep	kept	kept

base verb	simple past	past participle
know	knew	known
lay	laid	laid
leave	left	left
lose	lost	lost
make	made	made
mean	meant	meant
meet	met	met
overtake	overtook	overtaken
pay	paid	paid
put	put	put
read	read	read
ride	rode	ridden
ring	rang	rung
run	ran	run
say	said	said
see	saw	seen
sell	sold	sold
send	sent	sent
shine	shone	shone
sing	sang	sung
sit	sat	sat
sleep	slept	slept
speak	spoke	spoken
spend	spent	spent
stand	stood	stood
steal	stole	stolen
swim	swam	swum
take	took	taken
teach	taught	taught
tell	told	told
think	thought	thought
throw	threw	thrown
understand	understood	understood
wake up	woke up	woken up
wear	wore	worn
win	won	won
write	wrote	written

UNIT 2 GRAMMAR 2

Page 23, Exercise 8

Fri	class trip Science Museum 3 p.m.
Sat	visit grandpa 7 p.m.
Sun	ice skating 11 a.m. meet Emma to finish art project 4 p.m.
Mon	French test 9:15 a.m.
Tue	judo lesson 6:15 p.m.

UNIT 3 GRAMMAR 2

Page 35, Exercise 7

UNIT 5 LISTENING AND VOCABULARY

Page 56, Exercise 8

1 In which country is the Eiffel Tower? (France)
2 What nationality was the astronaut Neil Armstrong? (American)
3 Berlin is the capital city of which country? (Germany)
4 Which nationality were the writers Tolstoy and Dostoevsky? (Russian)
5 Which language do you write from right to left? (Arabic)
6 Which country's flag is red with one big yellow star and four little stars? (China)

UNIT 2 GRAMMAR 2

Page 23, Exercise 8

Fri	guitar lesson 4:20 p.m.
	Sal's party 7 p.m.
Sat	go shopping with Tom 10:30 a.m.
Sun	meet cousins at bus station 11:45 a.m.
	study for math test 5:30 p.m.
Mon	math test 10:30 a.m.
Tue	go to dentist 4 p.m.

UNIT 3 GRAMMAR 2

Page 35, Exercise 7

UNIT 5 LISTENING AND VOCABULARY

Page 56, Exercise 8

1 Name two countries where people speak Spanish. (Spain, Mexico)
2 Hô Chi Minh is the capital city of which country? (Vietnam)
3 Which country's flag is white with a red circle? (Japan)
4 What nationality are the soccer players Ronaldo and Ronaldinho? (Brazilian)
5 In which country is the Tower of Pisa? (Italy)
6 What nationality was the artist Frida Kahlo? (Mexican)

Move Beyond 3

WORKBOOK

macmillan education

Nina Lauder
Ingrid Wisniewska

Macmillan Education
4 Crinan Street
London N1 9XW
A division of Macmillan Publishers Limited

Companies and representatives throughout the world

ISBN 978-1-380-00771-1

Written by Nina Lauder and Ingrid Wisniewska

Go Beyond First published 2015
First edition entitled *Beyond* published 2014

Designed by EMC Design Ltd.

Illustrated by Peter Cornwell p. 115 (top); Cyrus Deboo pp. 70, 121, 132; Stephen Dew pp. 115 (br), 134; Mark Duffin p. 71; Sally Elford pp. 88 (except ice skates), 113; Kevin Hopgood pp. 67, 68, 103, 107; Bob Lea pp. 76, 78, 131 (cr); Roger Stewart (Beehive Illustration) pp. 81, 111; Tony Wilkins pp. 83, 95, 131 (bl), 135.

Cover design by EMC Design Ltd.
Cover photograph by Getty Images/F1online/parasola parasola
Picture research by Tessa Hammond and Emily Taylor

The authors and publishers would like to thank the following for permission to reproduce their images:

Alamy/Built Images/Darren Setlon p. 84(d), Alamy/Cultura RM p. 100(2), Alamy/Heather Gail Delaney p. 75(a), Alamy/Gary Dublanko p. 84(a), Alamy/Mark Dyball p. 114, Alamy/Mike Hill p. 99(a), Alamy/Image Source pp. 79(3), 89, Alamy/Hilary Morgan p. 84(c), Alamy/Rolf Nussbaumer Photography p. 100(3), Alamy/Papilio p. 100(4), Alamy/PhotoAlto p. 82, Alamy/Mark Richardson p. 84(b);
BananaStock p. 69;
Brand X p. 100(1);
Corbis p. 100(6), Corbis/IDC/amanaimages p. 118, Corbis/Eric Audras/PhotoAlto p. 126(tl), Corbis/Tanya Constantine/Blend Images p. 79(1), Corbis/Bruce Damonte/Arcaid p. 84(e), Corbis/Jamie Grill/Blend Images p. 129, Corbis/Hill Street Studios/Blend Images p. 130(b), Corbis/Igor E./Image Source p. 76, Corbis/Inspirestock p. 130(m), Corbis/PT Images/Tetra Images p. 67, Corbis/Radius Images p. 138, Corbis/RelaXimages p. 132(r), Corbis/Inti St Clair/Blend Images p. 112(bm), Corbis/Rudy Sulgan p. 86, Corbis/Art Wolfe/Mint Images p. 100(5);
Digital Vision p. 99(b);
Getty Images/All Canada Photos p. 75(c), Getty Images/Blend Images p. 106, Getty Images/Nivek Neslo/Photodisc p. 77(cr), Getty Images/Cultura pp. 79(2), 98, Getty Images/E+ p. 74, Getty Images/Fuse/Thinkstock Images p. 62, Getty Images/Future Publishing p. 77(br), Getty Images/Image Source pp. 130(t), 132(l), Getty Images/Ron Levine p. 126(tr), Getty Images/Moment/Kristian Bell p. 99(c), Getty Images/Photodisc/Derek Latta p. 132(m), Getty Images/Tim Robberts/Digital Vision p. 135, Getty Images/Gregor Schuster p. 75(b), Getty Images/Anup Shah p. 96, Getty Images/Robin Skjoldborg p. 70(br), Getty Images/Stockbyte p. 84(br), Getty Images/Photographer's Choice/David C Tomlinson p. 84(f);
Plain Picture/Cristopher Civitillo p. 108(br), Plain Picture/Design Pics p. 101, Plain Picture/Glasshouse p. 87, Plain Picture/Maskot p. 108(tl), Plain Picture/PhotoAlto p. 119, Plain Picture/Score by Aflo p. 70(cr);
SuperStock/View Pictures Ltd p. 90;
Thinkstock/Goodshoot p. 85, Thinkstock/iStock/Natasha Litova p. 88(tr).

Printed and bound in China

2021 2020 2019 2018 2017
10 9 8 7 6 5 4 3 2 1

CONTENTS

S A DAY IN DYLAN'S LIFE

VOCABULARY 1 >>> Routines, family, clothes, and school things

1 Label the things in the school bags with the words in the box.

class schedule keys lunchbox notebook pencil case textbook

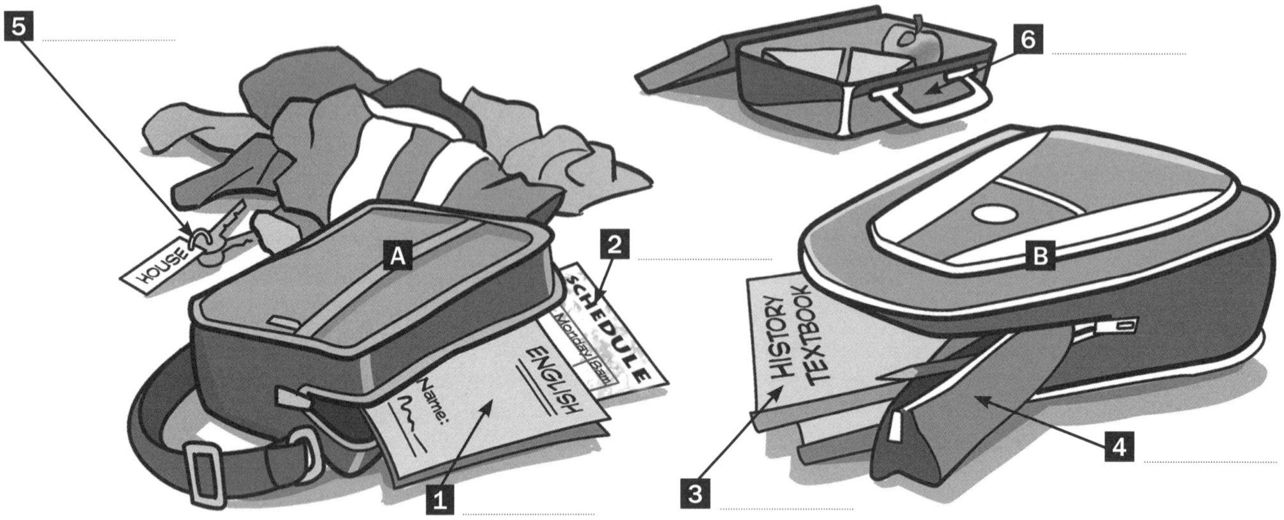

2 Look at the school bags in Exercise 1 and answer the questions.

1 Is there a notebook in bag A? *Yes, there is.*
2 Is there a class schedule in bag A?
3 Is there a pencil case in bag A?
4 Are there any textbooks in bag B?
5 Is there a lunchbox in bag B?
6 Are there any keys in bag B?

3 Choose the correct options to complete the text about Melanie's family.

Hi! My name's Melanie, and I'm twelve years old. I don't have any sisters, but I have a little (1) ***sister / brother***. His name's Lee and he's five. We live with my (2) ***mom and dad / brother and sister*** in a house in Hawaii. My (3) ***grandparents / sisters*** live near our house, so I sometimes visit them after school. My mom's sister, my (4) ***uncle / aunt*** Teresa, also lives in our neighborhood. She doesn't have any children, but my uncle and aunt on the island of Maui have two: my (5) ***cousins / brothers*** Brendan and Darren! We visit them every summer.

4 a Choose the correct options from the box below to complete the text.

Raul wakes up at eight o'clock, but he doesn't (1) ____ until 8:05. First he goes to the bathroom to (2) ____ , and then he goes back to his bedroom to (3) ____ for school. He normally wears jeans and a T-shirt to school, but it's cold today, so he's taking a (4) ____ too. After that he (5) ____ in the kitchen with his dad and his sisters. After breakfast he packs his (6) ____ . He needs to take a lot of textbooks to school today! At 8:40 he (7) ____ by bus with his sisters. They (8) ____ at 8:55 – just in time!

1	a	get up	b	go to bed
2	a	pack his school bag	b	brush his teeth
3	a	get dressed	b	get up
4	a	sweatshirt	b	skirt
5	a	wakes up	b	has breakfast
6	a	school bag	b	lunch box
7	a	goes to school	b	gets out of school
8	a	get dressed	b	get to school

b Write two sentences about what you do before school.

5 a 68 Listen to Eva and Joanna talking about clothes for school. Check (✓) the items of clothing you hear in the table.

pants	jeans	shirt	sweatshirt	shoes	sneakers	skirt	dress
			✓				

b Think of two more items of clothing.

GRAMMAR 1 *be, have, there is / there are*

Before school

S

1 Complete the grammar tables with the correct forms.

Verb: *be*		
I	'm (1) (..........) / 'm not (am not)	12 years old.
He, She, It	's (is) / (2) .... (is not)	from Mexico.
You, We, They	're (3) (..........) / (4) .... (are not)	happy.

Verb: *have*		
I, You, We, They	(5) .... / don't have	three brothers.
He, She, It	has / (6)	two sisters.

2 ▶69 Listen and match the conversations to the pictures. Write the correct number.

A ☐

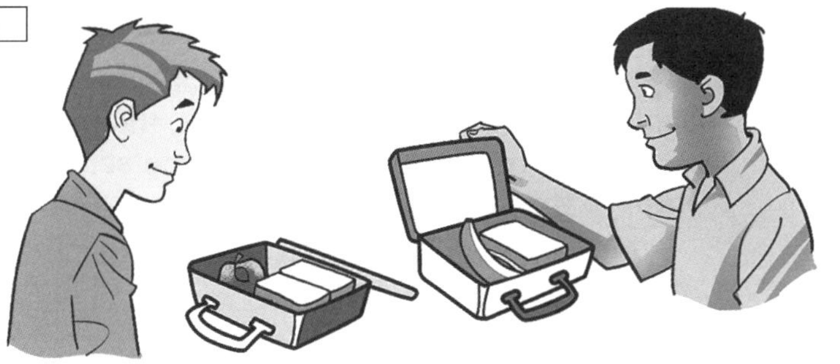

B ☐

C ☐

3 Choose the correct options to complete the conversations.

1 **Dad:** Matt, hurry up! You (1) ***has*** / ***have*** five minutes!
Matt: Oh no – I (2) ***doesn't*** / ***don't*** have my house key!
Dad: (3) ***There's*** / ***There are*** a key on the table near the door.
Matt: OK, thanks! See you later!

2 **Felipe:** What (4) ***'s*** / ***'re*** in your lunchbox today?
Matt: Two cheese sandwiches and an apple.
Felipe: Do you (5) ***has*** / ***have*** any chocolate?
Matt: No, I (6) ***doesn't*** / ***don't***.

3 **Mr. Andrews:** Matt, you (7) ***'s*** / ***'re*** 10 minutes late!
Matt: I (8) ***'s*** / ***'m*** sorry!
Mr. Andrews: Do you (9) ***have*** / ***has*** your homework?
Matt: Yes, I (10) ***does*** / ***do***. Here it (11) ***is*** / ***are***.
Mr. Andrews: Good! Now sit down and open your book.

4 Complete the sentences with the correct form of *be* or *have*.

1 I .... three English books.
2 There .... two pens in my bag.
3 I .... 13 years old.
4 There .... a class schedule on the wall.
5 Ella .... a lunchbox.
6 We .... a nice teacher.
7 Your keys .... on the table.
8 Ali .... a new textbook.

5 Write the sentences using the correct form of *have*.

1 Sarah / three sisters.
Sarah has three sisters.
2 I / my homework. (not)
....
3 You / much time. (not)
....
4 They / new bicycles.
....
5 We / our textbooks. (not)
....
6 Judy / her lunchbox. (not)
....

6 Check (✓) the correct answer for you. Then complete the sentences.

Do you have a brother?
☐ **Yes, I have .... brother(s).**
☐ **No, I ....**

Do you have a sister?
☐ **Yes, I have .... sister(s).**
☐ **No, I ....**

Is there a book in your school bag today?
☐ **Yes. There .... book(s).**
☐ **No, there ....**

VOCABULARY 2

Classroom phrases, free-time activities

1 Match the phrases to complete the sentences.

1	Open your books	a	the question.
2	Can you	b	to the bathroom?
3	Can I please go	c	repeat that, please?
4	I don't understand	d	*padre* in English?
5	How do you say	e	Exercise 8.
6	For homework, do	f	to page 14.

2 a Complete the questions and sentences in Exercise 1 with "?" or "."

b Write one more classroom expression.

....

3 a Solve the code and complete the sentences.

A	B	C	D	E	F	G	H	I	J	K	L	M	N	O	P	Q	R	S	T	U	V	W	X	Y	Z
26	25	24	23	22	21	20	19	18	17	16	15	14	13	12	11	10	9	8	7	6	5	4	3	2	1

1 He likes

8	4	18	14	14	18	13	20

.

He goes every Friday with his friends. ☐

2 She likes

26	24	7	18	13	20

and singing. She's very good! ☐

3 I

23	12		19	12	14	22	4	12	9	16

in my bedroom after dinner. ☐

4 "Do you like

24	12	12	16	18	13	20

?"

"I do! I'm only a beginner, though!" ☐

5 I sometimes

9	22	26	23		26		25	12	12	16

after school. ☐

6 I like sports! I

11	15	26	2		7	22	13	13	18	8

every Monday and Wednesday. ☐

7 I like

15	18	8	7	22	13	18	13	20

7	12		14	6	8	18	24

,

especially hip hop. ☐

8 She likes languages. She can

8	11	22	26	16		22	13	20	15	18	8	19

well. ☐

b Check (✓) the activities you like doing.

4 (70) Listen to three girls talking about what they like and don't like doing. Complete the table with a check (✓) or an X (✗). Then read the sentences and choose the correct option (*Tanya, Leah, Nora*).

	Tanya	Leah	Nora
Speaking Spanish			
Listening to music	✓		
Reading			
Acting			
Cooking			
Swimming			

1 She likes speaking Spanish, but she doesn't like cooking or swimming. *Tanya*
2 She doesn't like cooking, but she likes listening to music and acting. ....
3 She likes swimming and reading. She doesn't like speaking Spanish. ....
4 She likes listening to music and reading, but she doesn't like acting. ....
5 She likes acting, but she doesn't like cooking. ....
6 She doesn't like listening to music, but she likes cooking. ....

5 a Complete the sentences with activities from Exercise 3.

1 She likes *swimming* and goes to the pool every day.
2 Enrique is in the drama club. He likes .... and wants to go to Hollywood one day.
3 Teresa loves languages. She likes .... when she can, so she goes to classes twice a week.
4 My brother doesn't like .... books, but he likes comic books and magazines.
5 My best friend likes .... in her bedroom every evening. She listens to her favorite band.
6 Do you like .... ? I love making new things in the kitchen.

b Write two more after-school activities.

....

GRAMMAR 2 *Wh-* questions, *like* + *-ing*

After school

1 Complete the grammar tables with the correct forms.

Wh-* questions with *be			
Question word	***Be***	**Subject**	**Examples**
Where / What / What time / Who / When / Why / How / How old / How long	am	I?	Where am I?
	(1) ______	he? she? it?	When (2) ______ it?
	(3) ______	you? we? they?	How (4) ______ you? Who (5) ______ they? Where (6) ______ your notebooks? How (7) ______ your brothers? (8) ______ are your favorite sports?

***Wh-* questions with other verbs**				
Question word	***Do***	**Subject**	**Main verb**	**Examples**
Where What What time Who When Why How How old How long	(9) ______	I (10) ______ we they	get up?	When (11) ______ we start school? What subjects (12) ______ you hate? Where (13) ______ she play tennis? What (14) ______ they do after school?
	(15) ______	(16) ______ she it	live?	When (17) ______ school end? (18) ______ music does she like? (19) ______ does he like computer games? How (20) ______ does the movie last?

JUDO CLUB
Stay fit and have fun!

Monday 4:00–6:00 p.m.
- Main gym
- Wear comfortable clothes
- Teacher: Tony Nakagawa

2 a Choose the correct options to complete the questions.

1 ***What*** / ***Where*** is the judo club?
2 ***Who*** / ***What*** do you wear?
3 ***Who*** / ***What*** is the teacher?
4 ***Where*** / ***When*** does it start?
5 ***What*** / ***Why*** do people do judo?
6 ***How long*** / ***When*** does the lesson last?

a Comfortable clothes.
b Tony Nakagawa.
c Two hours.
d To stay fit and have fun.
e In the gym.
f 4:00 p.m.

b Match the questions (1–6) to the answers (a–f).

3 Complete the sentences with information from the table.

					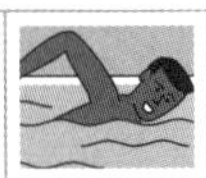
Allie	😐	😐	😠	🙂	🙁
Bob	😠	😐	🙁	🙂	🙂
Katie	🙂	😐	🙁	😐	😠

Key: 🙂 = love 😐 = like 🙁 = not like 😠 = hate

1 Allie loves ______ .
2 Bob hates ______ .
3 Katie likes ______ and ______ .
4 Allie doesn't like ______ .
5 Bob likes ______ .
6 Katie hates ______ .
7 Bob doesn't like ______ .
8 Katie loves ______ .

My name's Kyla. I'm 13 years old. I live in Florida. I have one sister and one brother. I go to judo club after school every Monday. It starts at 4:00 p.m. and ends at 6:00 p.m. My judo teacher's name is Tony. After judo, I go home and have dinner. In my free time, I like playing soccer and tennis and chatting with friends online.

4 Read the paragraph to the right and make questions about Kyla.

1 *What's her name*? Kyla.
2 ______? Thirteen.
3 ______? Florida.
4 ______? To judo club.
5 ______? Playing soccer and tennis.

1 SWITCH ON

UNIT

VOCABULARY 1 »» Applications (apps)

1 Choose the correct options to complete the text.

I love technology because it changes all the time! For example, I don't use a (1) ***television*** / ***camera*** to watch movies because I don't have one in my bedroom. I play DVDs on my game (2) ***computer*** / ***console*** at home and on my sister's (3) ***cell*** / ***laptop*** when we go on trips. I don't have a (4) ***laptop*** / ***game console*** because I share my sister's. I have a really old (5) ***computer*** / ***console*** in my bedroom for doing homework. For my birthday, I want a new (6) ***MP3 player*** / ***smartphone*** so I can make phone calls *and* play videos and music. Or I'd like a (7) ***tablet*** / ***television*** – for music, videos, games, and homework. They're very expensive, though.

2 Rearrange the letters to label each app.

a rallcucota ……………

b lendcara ……………

c creaam ……………

d sapscom ……………

e megas ……………

f laim ……………

g spam ……………

h sneot ……………

i eodivs ……………

j sagessem ……………

3 Complete the sentences with apps from Exercise 2.

BUY THE LATEST APPLICATIONS IN OUR FANTASTIC APP STORE! USE OUR APPS ON YOUR LAPTOP, PHONE, OR TABLET.

Use the (1) …………… app to remember your class times and all your friends' birthdays.
Use the (2) …………… app to write down ideas for songs and stories.
Use the (3) …………… app to get letters from friends around the world.
Use the (4) …………… app to check your direction.
Use the (5) …………… app to check how much you spend.
Use the (6) …………… app to update your friends quickly.
Use the (7) …………… app to edit and store your photos online.
Use the (8) …………… app to check where things are.
Use the (9) …………… app to play cards.
Use the (10) …………… app to watch your favorite pop stars on stage.

4 Which apps are fun? Which apps are useful? Which apps can be both? Write them in the chart.

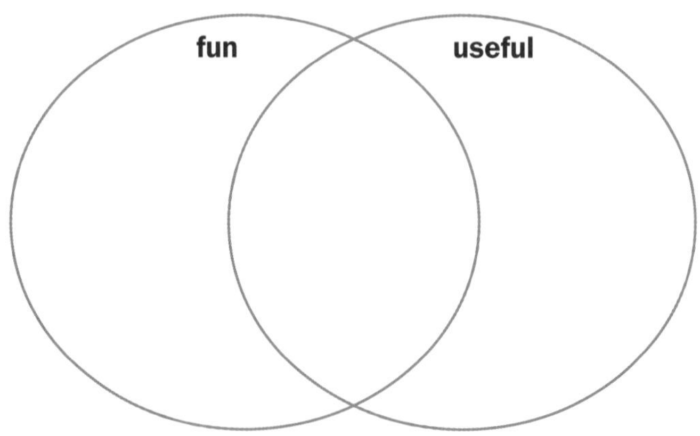

5 Complete the activities with the words in the box.

internet   on   online   social networking site   videos   web browser

1 use a ……………
2 open a ……………
3 chat ……………
4 log ……………
5 surf the ……………
6 watch ……………

1 Complete the tips with the words in the box.

REMEMBER HOW TO …

understand new words

adjective	before	compare	similar	type

1 Identify the ______ of word (verb, noun, ______, adverb).

2 ______ it to your language. Is there a ______ word? Does its meaning help you?

3 Look at the words and sentences ______ and after the new word.

2 Match the words in bold to the sentences (a–d).

1 Our brains use a lot of **energy**.

2 It's important to take time to sit down and **relax**.

a It's a verb. ______

b It means something similar to *power*. ______

c It's a noun. ______

d It means something similar to *rest*. ______

3 Read the magazine article. What's the main topic?

a the dangers of texting

b new technology for texting

c why teens like to text

9:30

TEXTING TEENS :) <3 #

Recent surveys show a dramatic increase in the amount of texting by teenagers. One survey says that more than 66 percent of teenagers own a cell phone, and they send about 190 texts per week! Some teenagers send hundreds of texts a day. In fact, many teenagers spend so much time texting, they can't imagine life without their cell phone.

So why do teenagers like texting? What makes it better than phone calls? Many teens say that texting is easier, faster, and more fun. Texts are private. Teenagers can send texts during class time and no one can hear what they're saying. Texts are cheap. On a lot of phone plans you can have unlimited texts, so it makes no difference if you send one text or a hundred texts, the cost is the same.

Teenagers also say that texting is the best way to stay in touch with friends. When they feel lonely or sad, they can talk to their friends any time. Teens say it's nice to get texts from friends because it helps them feel relaxed if they are nervous or depressed. Texting has a negative side too. Too much texting can make your thumbs hurt!

4 Decide if these statements are correct (*C*), incorrect (*I*), or if the text doesn't say (*DS*).

1 Teenagers are texting more than before. ______

2 Many teenagers send a hundred texts per hour. ______

3 Many teenagers feel their phones are a necessary part of their lives. ______

4 Teenagers often send texts to their parents. ______

5 Teenagers have very high phone bills. ______

6 Texting makes teenagers feel relaxed. ______

5 Look at the underlined words in the text. Write the type of word next to each word below. Use *noun*, *verb*, or *adjective*. Circle words that are similar in your language.

1 survey	noun	5 unlimited	______
2 dramatic	______	6 nervous	______
3 imagine	______	7 depressed	______
4 private	______	8 thumbs	______

6 Choose the best meaning for the words from Exercise 5. Then circle which tip(s) in Exercise 1 helped you.

1 survey
a study b quiz
Tip 1 2 3

2 dramatic
a loud b big
Tip 1 2 3

3 imagine
a describe b think of
Tip 1 2 3

4 private
a personal b easy
Tip 1 2 3

5 unlimited
a as many as you want b extra
Tip 1 2 3

6 nervous
a worried b quiet
Tip 1 2 3

7 depressed
a sad b lost
Tip 1 2 3

8 thumbs
a part of face b part of hand
Tip 1 2 3

MOVE BEYOND

Use the internet to find an English article about one of your hobbies or favorite ways to relax. Use the tips in Exercise 1 to help you understand the article.

GRAMMAR 1 Simple present, adverbs, and expressions of frequency

Talk about how often you do things

1 Complete the grammar tables with the correct forms.

Simple present – affirmative			
I, You, We, (1) ______	sometimes (2) ______	computer games.	
He, (3) ______, It	plays	computer games	now and then.
Simple present – negative			
I, You, We, (4) ______	don't play	computer games.	
He, (5) ______, It	(6) ______ play	computer games.	

Simple present – questions				Answers
How often	(7) ______	I, you, we, they	(8) ______ computer games?	Once a week. Hardly ever.
	does	(9) ______, she, it		
Simple present – *yes/no* questions				**Answers**
Do	I, you, we, they	(10) ______	computer games?	Yes, I do. No, we (11) ______.
(12) ______	he, she, it			Yes, she does. No, he (13) ______.

2 Choose the correct options to complete the rules. Use the tables in Exercise 1 to help you.

Simple present

1 Use the simple present to write about ***routines* / *plans***.
2 To form the ***first* / *third*** person singular form of the simple present, add *-s*, *-es*, or *-ies* to the verb.
3 Use *don't* and *doesn't* ***before* / *after*** the verb to form simple present negatives.
4 Use ***have* and *has* / *do* and *does*** to form simple present questions.

Adverbs and expressions of frequency

5 Adverbs go ***before* / *after*** main verbs and after *be* and *can*.
6 Expressions of frequency (e.g., *now and then*) go ***in the middle* / *at the beginning or the end*** of a sentence.

3 Write the third person singular form of these verbs in the correct column.

do fly go play ~~send~~ study teach use

-s	-es	-ies
sends		

4 Use some of the verbs in Exercise 3 to complete the sentences. Are they habits and routines (*H* and *R*) or things that are generally true (*T*)?

1 Susan rarely ______ email. ______
2 Rafael Nadal ______ tennis really well! ______
3 Sasha ______ Spanish on Saturdays because she's going to Mexico on vacation. ______
4 He ______ people to play the guitar on weekends. ______
5 Eddy always ______ to Costa Rica from Miami International Airport. ______
6 Gina ______ to her best friend's house every Saturday. ______

5 Number the adverbs in order from 1 (0%) to 7 (100%).

☐ almost always ☐ always ☐ usually ☐ hardly ever ☐ never ☐ often ☐ sometimes

6 › **Choose the correct option from the box below to complete the conversation.**

Ivan: How often (1) ____ check your email?
Linda: Oh, I (2) ____ check it very often, maybe three or four times a week. My sister (3) ____ a lot of emails to her friends every day. But I (4) ____ too busy! How about you?
Ivan: I check (5) ____ , but I hardly ever (6) ____ email. I prefer texting. I (7) ____ a hundred messages in a day!
Linda: That's amazing. I guess you (8) ____ a lot of friends!

1	a do you	b you do
2	a doesn't	b don't
3	a send	b sends
4	a usually am	b am usually
5	a my email occasionally	b occasionally my email
6	a send	b sends
7	a sometimes send	b send sometimes
8	a have	b has

7 › **Rearrange the words to make questions.**

1 you / every day / Do / chat online ?
Do you chat online every day?
2 does / How often / send email / Steve ?
3 play music / Does / your phone ?
4 normally / you / on a console / Do / play games ?
5 watch DVDs / does / your family / How often ?
6 have / your laptop / a camera / Does ?

8 ›› **Use the prompts to write questions. Then use the words in parentheses to write answers.**

1 you / chat online
Q: How often *do you chat online* ?
A: (not often) *I don't often chat online* .
2 she / update her blog
Q: How often ____ ?
A: (from time to time) ____ .
3 your friends / check their email
Q: How often ____ ?
A: (regularly) ____ .
4 Leo and Vicky / post photos online
Q: How often ____ ?
A: (hardly ever) ____ .
5 your parents / send you text messages
Q: How often ____ ?
A: (every day) ____ .
6 your computer / crash
Q: How often ____ ?
A: (not often) ____ .

9 ››› **Rewrite the sentences with no mistakes.**

1 He don't send often email.
He doesn't often send email.
2 I checks every day my email.
3 She in the mornings study online.
4 How you does chat online often?
How often
5 Regularly does you update your blog?
6 I haven't often problems with my cell phone.
I don't
7 They from time to time go online.
8 You do talk to friends on your cell phone sometimes?

LISTENING

Listen for the main ideas

1 Label the devices.

A

d _ _ _ _ _ l c _ _ _ _ a

pictures

B

c _ _ _ p _ _ _ e

C

t _ _ _ _ t

2 Which words do you associate with each device? Write them under photos A, B, and C. You can use the words more than once.

album   file   menu   number   pictures   save
screen   speakers   USB port   view   watch

3 (▶71) Listen to three short conversations. Which device (cell phone, digital camera, or tablet) are the people talking about?

Conversation 1 is about the ________ .
Conversation 2 is about the ________ .
Conversation 3 is about the ________ .

4 (▶71) Listen to the conversations again. Did you hear any words from Exercise 2? Use them to complete the table.

Conversation 1	*pictures*
Conversation 2	*screen*
Conversation 3	

5 Use the information in Exercises 2–4 to explain the problems in the conversations.

Conversation 1 ________
Conversation 2 ________
Conversation 3 ________

6 (▶71) Listen again. In which conversation did you hear the phrases below? Write *1*, *2*, or *3* to match the conversation to the phrase. Write *X* if you don't hear the phrase.

____ Great!
____ Excuse me.
____ No problem.
____ Oh, I see.
____ Oh, thanks.
____ Just a second.
____ Thanks a lot.
____ What did you say?
____ What is it?
____ What's wrong?

VOCABULARY 2

Computer parts

1 Complete the crossword.

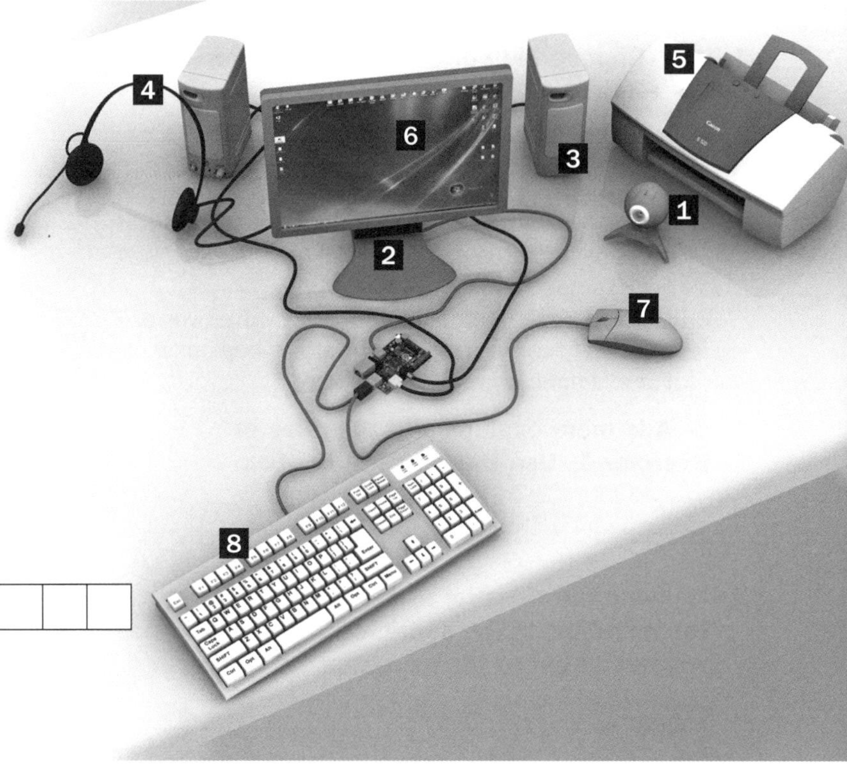

2 Write the names of the computer parts.

1 It's small. I move it around my desk. ___
2 It's round. It looks at me. ___
3 It's gray. It's a rectangle. It has letters and numbers. ___
4 It's a place to put in my memory stick/phone charger. ___ ___
5 It's attached to the headphones. I speak into it. ___

3 Complete the text with the words in the box.

blog	chat	computer	invention	log on	post
screen	text messages	webcam	website		

We learn a lot about technology in my (1) ___ class at school. This week we're learning how to (2) ___ to the class website and (3) ___ messages onto the class (4) ___. We sometimes use Skype™ to (5) ___ online with students from our partner school in Mexico. We practice Spanish, and they practice English! We send (6) ___ or we use the (7) ___, so we can see other students on the (8) ___ when we talk to them. It's really fun. I think the internet is such a cool (9) ___! Next semester I want to learn to make my own (10) ___!

END CALL STOP VIDEO

WORDS & BEYOND

Choose the correct option to complete the sentences.

1 They ___ the internet every night.
  a connect
  b surf
  c create
2 How many ___ do you have on your desktop?
  a ads
  b messages
  c icons
3 Our house has two different internet ___.
  a connections
  b appliances
  c screens
4 Do you need a password to ___?
  a switch off
  b write code
  c log on
5 Sasha knows how to ___ code.
  a send
  b make
  c write
6 A tablet is a really useful type of ___.
  a computer
  b connection
  c app

GRAMMAR 2 Articles: *a/an* and *the*

Use *a/an* and *the* to refer to things

1 a › Choose the correct option to complete the rules (1–3).

1 Use ***a*** / ***an*** before countable nouns that start with a consonant sound.
For example: *computer*, ________ , ________
2 Use ***a*** / ***an*** before countable nouns that start with a vowel sound.
For example: *office*, ________ . ________
3 Use ***a*** / ***an*** before nouns that start with a vowel but don't have a vowel sound at the beginning.
For example: *university*, ________ , ________

b Add more examples to the rules in Exercise 1. Use the words in the box.

app cell phone Euro hotel umbrella unit

2 ›› Read the rules for using *the*. Then correct the mistakes in the sentences. Write the rule you used next to the sentence.

Rules
1 Use *the* before something already mentioned.
2 Use *the* before the only example of a thing.
3 Use *the* before superlatives.
4 Don't use *the* before names of days.
5 Don't use *the* before plural items that aren't specific.
6 Don't use *the* before singular place names.

a I love the computers.
Rule: *5 I love computers.*
b I live in the New Zealand.
Rule: ________
c I use internet every day.
Rule: ________
d This is best cell phone you can buy.
Rule: ________
e We have computer class on the Thursdays.
Rule: ________
f I go to school in a big city. School has 2,000 students.
Rule: ________

3 ›› Write the words in the correct column in the chart.

April Australia best internet January Main Street moon Netherlands sun Tuesday United Nations

zero article (–)	*the*

4 ›› Choose the correct options to complete the text.

My name is Gisela, and I'm (1) ***a*** / ***the*** student at (2) ***a*** / **–** school in (3) ***the*** / **–** Seattle, Washington. For me, (4) ***the*** / ***a*** best class of the week is computer graphics. We have (5) **–** / ***a*** really good teacher, and I love learning how to make (6) ***the*** / **–** animations and comic books. We also have (7) ***an*** / **–** extra class on (8) **–** / ***the*** Fridays, during (9) ***a*** / ***the*** lunch break. I want to be (10) **–** / ***a*** graphic designer one day.

5 ››› Complete the text with *a*, *an*, *the*, or zero article (–).

TECHNOLOGY REVIEWS **NEW**

This is (1) ________ new tablet from Jetset Electronics, and it's (2) ________ smallest one on the market right now. It has (3) ________ great screen and it has (4) ________ two cameras, one at the front and one at the back. It's very easy to download (5) ________ my apps onto it. I use it a lot on (6) ________ train, and (7) ________ battery lasts for a very long time. This is (8) ________ excellent device for all kinds of online activities – reading books, surfing (9) ________ web, and watching (10) ________ videos.

SPEAKING

Ask for and give opinions

1 a What is each device for? Label each picture with the best answer from the phrases in the box. Choose one answer for each picture.

cleaning the floor | having fun | making calls | ~~reading books~~ | taking pictures

reading books
useful,

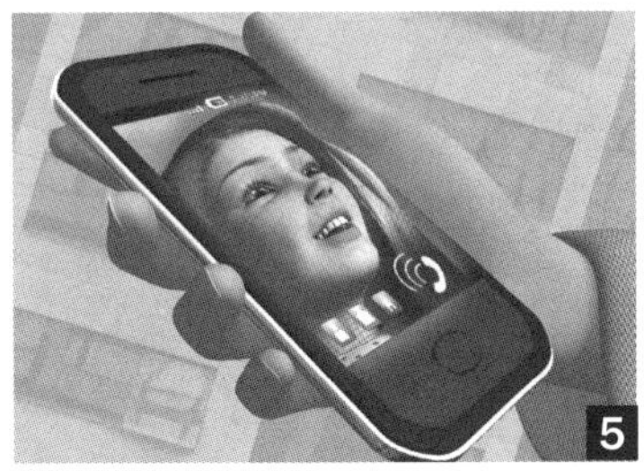

b What do you think about these devices? Write two adjectives below each picture (for example, *boring*, *creative*, *exciting*, *silly*, *ugly*, *useful*).

2 ▶72 Read the conversation and complete the phrases for asking or giving opinions. Then listen and check your answers.

Annie: What (1) ______ think about this new e-reader, Nick?

Nick: (2) ______ it's very useful. It's small and it isn't heavy. You can use it to read books on the train.

Annie: I agree. I think it's very useful because you don't need a lot of heavy books. But look at this wrist camera; it's a really creative idea. You can take pictures anywhere!

Nick: I'd love to have one, but (3) ______ think it's expensive? It costs a lot of money!

Annie: I don't (4) ______ . (5) ______ do you think about this house robot? I don't think it's very interesting. It's so ugly.

Nick: Oh, I disagree. I think (6) ______ cool. I hate housework!

Annie: Look at this computer pet. Now that's really silly! Who wants that?

Nick: Oh … yeah, I see what you mean … kind of stupid. But here's something that's really creative. You can see people and images in 3D. It looks like they're real!

Annie: Yes, that's really amazing.

3 ▶72 Listen to the conversation again. What do Annie and Nick think about the devices? Complete the table with the correct adjectives.

Gadget	Nick's opinion	Annie's opinion
e-reader		
wrist camera		
house robot		
computer pet		
3D phone		

4 a PRONOUNCE Which words have the sound /æ/ in them? Complete the table with the words in the box.

calculator | calendar | camera | compass | games | laptop | mail | maps | messages | tablet

Words with /æ/	Words without /æ/
calculator	

b ▶73 Listen and check your answers. Practice repeating the words.

Use the correct word order

1 Look at the underlined words in each sentence. What type of words are they?

adjective   adverb   ~~verb~~   object   subject   verb

1 I surf the web to find new games. *verb*
2 My cell phone helps me organize my time. ....
3 I often download music from the internet. ....
4 I know a really good site for sharing photos. ....
5 My friends send me text messages every day. ....
6 I often send text messages to my friends. ....

2 Read the blog below and find three examples of the following:

1 adjectives ...., ..., ...
2 adverbs of frequency ...., ..., ...
3 expressions of frequency ...., ..., ...
4 subject/verb/object pattern ...., ..., ...

QUESTION: What do you like doing most on the internet?

I hang out with friends. I chat online or visit social networking sites. I never feel lonely because I'm always in touch with friends. I get a lot of texts and email from my friends every day. We share music tips, photos, and videos. I almost never talk on the phone.

I like playing games online. Sometimes I play with virtual friends and sometimes with real friends from school. There are a lot of new games, but we often play old games too. I usually play free games, but now and then I pay for a game, and it's not too expensive.

I love shopping online. Sometimes I buy clothes or CDs. I can get the latest things online, and it's fast to get them too. I don't mind waiting for the clothes to arrive, and the price is usually cheaper. I go to the mall from time to time – but usually only to window shop.

3 Rearrange the words to make sentences.

1 social networking sites / visit / I / sometimes .
....
2 hardly ever / computer games / buys / She .
....
3 We / online / shop / often .
....
4 usually / text messages / Elisa / sends .
....
5 games / every weekend / I / play .
....

4 Write three sentences about each person on the right. Use the information below the photos to help you.

✗ = never   ✓ = hardly ever
✓✓ = sometimes   ✓✓✓ = often

1 *Ali often texts her friends.*
....
....
2 ....
....
....
3 ....
....
....

1 Ali

text my friends ✓✓✓
play games ✓✓
chat online ✓

2 Leo

play games ✗
update my blog ✓
download music ✓✓✓

3 Mike

surf the web ✓✓
check my favorite social network ✓✓
share photos ✗

5 **Look at the text on page 16. What's your favorite thing to do online? Use the *Ideas box* and the *Writing plan* to help you prepare.**

IDEAS BOX

chat online check my favorite social network listen to music shop online send messages surf the web watch videos

WRITING PLAN

Make notes for your answer.

1 Think of your favorite thing to do online.

....

2 Why do you like this activity? Think of three reasons.
Reason 1 ....
Reason 2 ....
Reason 3 ....

3 Where do you usually do this activity? At school? At home?

....

4 How often do you do this activity?

Adverbs of frequency: always never sometimes usually occasionally rarely hardly ever
Expressions of frequency: from time to time now and then all the time every day

WRITE AND CHECK

6 **Write your answer. Check (✓) the stages in the plan.**

Use lists to help you organize your time

1 **Look at the text. Where is it from?** *Tom's p........r*

Weekend	School prom SATURDAY NIGHT at 6:00 p.m. - pick up suit from cleaner (closes at 1:00 p.m.!) - get there EARLY to put out chairs and pay the DJ*** Soccer practice Saturday (9:00-11:00 a.m. BE THERE ON TIME!) then stay for more soccer with James and Kieran (until 1:00 p.m.) LUNCH and VIDEO GAMES at Kieran's (to 4:00 p.m.) ***get money from bank Dad's birthday on Sunday! Birthday dinner at 7:00 p.m. (pick up cake in the morning) SWIMMING with Sally and Mark - Sunday morning Band practice for school concert Saturday and Sunday at noon
Monday	a.m. math test 4:00 p.m. swimming 6:00 p.m. SCHOOL CONCERT

2 **Is Tom's time organized? What problems are there with his plans? Write three problems in your notebook.**

3 **Reorganize Tom's planner in your notebook. Make a list first, then decide on the best order for him to do things.**

GET ORGANIZED

1 Look at the two pictures and complete the sentences.

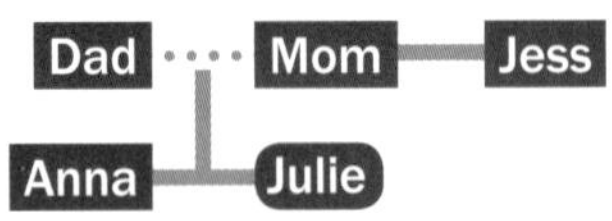

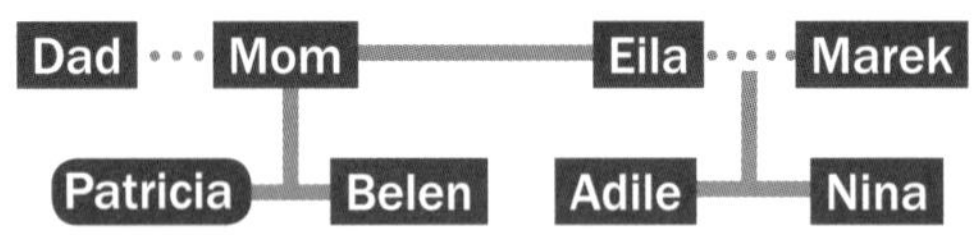

Clothes

1 Julie wears a s ________ r, j ________ , and sn ________ to school.
2 Patricia wears a sh ______ , a s ________ , and s ______ s to school.

School things

3 Julie has a n ______ book and a p ________ c ______ in her school bag.
4 Patricia has a te ________ , l ________ x, and c ______ p ______ in her school bag.

Free time

5 Julie likes l ________ g ______ m ______ and co ______ g in her free time.
6 Patricia likes t ______ g p ________ s and l ________ g Sp ______ h in her free time.

Family

7 Jess is Julie's ______ .
8 Adile and Nina are Patricia's ________ .

2 Read the clues and complete the crossword.

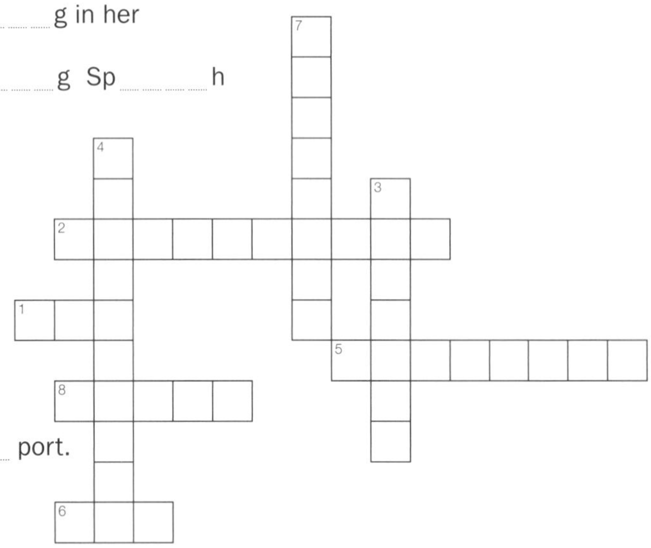

1 A ________ helps you find your way.
2 A ________ helps you solve a math problem.
3 A ________ shows you the right direction.
4 Use your ________ to listen to music on the train.
5 A ________ shows you the day and the date.
6 Connect a device to the computer using a ________ port.
7 Use your ________ to type the answer.
8 Use your ________ to click on the icon.

ALL ABOUT ME

1 What is your favorite way to communicate?

____

2 Name five apps that you regularly use on your phone.

____

____

3 What do you do to switch off?

____

1 Choose the correct options from the box below to complete the conversation.

Anna: You (1) ____ your homework on time, but I (2) ____ late! How (3) ____ organize your time?
Rick: Oh! That's a secret!
Anna: No, come on, tell me, please.
Rick: OK, well, at (4) ____ of each day, I make (5) ____ of all my homework. Then I number the things on the list in order.
Anna: I see. (6) ____ put the most important homework first?
Rick: No, I usually put (7) ____ homework first. I do the easy things later.
Anna: I see. I (8) ____ lists. Then on (9) ____ , I start to panic.
Rick: I don't panic. With my way I (10) ____ get stressed and everything is on time.
Anna: What a good idea!

1	**a**	finish always	**b**	always finish
2	**a**	am always	**b**	always am
3	**a**	you do	**b**	do you
4	**a**	the end	**b**	an end
5	**a**	a list	**b**	the list
6	**a**	Do you	**b**	You do
7	**a**	most difficult	**b**	the most difficult
8	**a**	make hardly ever	**b**	hardly ever make
9	**a**	Sunday	**b**	the Sunday
10	**a**	don't	**b**	doesn't

2 Choose the correct options to complete the paragraph.

At my school, there's (1) ***a*** / ***the*** computer room in (2) – / ***the*** library. We have (3) ***a*** / – computer class every day and we can use (4) ***a*** / ***the*** computers to go on (5) ***an*** / ***the*** internet. (6) – / ***The*** teacher gives us (7) ***a*** / – task and we have to complete (8) ***a*** / ***the*** task by (9) – / ***the*** end of (10) ***a*** / ***the*** class.

3 Complete the sentences with the correct forms of the verbs in the box.

buy chat play send ~~surf~~ watch

1 Danny likes *surfing* the internet. He usually *surfs* the internet during his lunch break.
2 Laura and Hannah enjoy ____________ computer games. They ____________ games every day.
3 I usually ____________ text messages to my friends. I don't like ____________ email.
4 We don't usually ____________ music CDs. We prefer ____________ music online.
5 Paula loves ____________ movies. She often ____________ movies on her laptop.
6 I like ____________ with my friends online. We sometimes ____________ for hours!

2 HOME AND AWAY

UNIT

VOCABULARY 1 »» Homes and household chores

1 a Complete the words with the correct vowels. Then match the rooms to the correct furniture and appliances. There are two matches for one of the rooms.

Rooms	Furniture/Appliances/ Other
1 b*a*thr*o* *o*m	a s__fa
2 b__dr__ __m	b s__ __ __e
3 k__tch__n	c b__d
4 l__v__ng r__ __m	d sh*o*w*e*r
5 d__n__ng r__ __m	e t__bl__
6 st__dy	f d__sk

b Write one more item found in each room.

1 *bathtub*
2 ……
3 ……
4 ……
5 ……
6 ……

2 Rearrange the letters to make different homes. Then complete the sentences with the words.

amentrtap bgalunow useho

1 My sister lives in New York City. She lives in a small …… on the fifth floor.
2 We live in a …… . All the rooms are on the first floor and there aren't any stairs.
3 My cousin lives in a …… in the countryside. It has two floors and a beautiful yard.

3 Read the clues. Complete the puzzle.

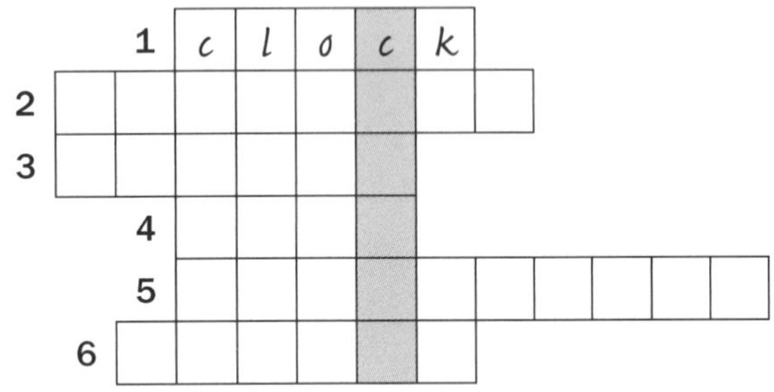

Clues:
1 this tells you what time it is
2 a comfortable seat
3 a place to wash in the bathroom
4 turn it on to read at night
5 you watch the news or movies on this
6 these help you see at night

Mystery word: (something that covers your floor)

……

4 a What is Jay doing? Complete the sentences with the correct verbs.

1 He *is mopping* the floor.

2 He …… the bed.

3 He …… the trash.

4 He …… the laundry.

5 He …… his room.

6 He …… the table.

7 He …… the ironing.

8 He …… the dishes.

b Check (✓) the things you do at home.

5 Find the odd word out in each group.

1	bathtub	shower	stove	sink
2	radio	television	computer	picture
3	hall	lamp	study	bedroom
4	door	cabinet	closet	refrigerator
5	sort the recycling	clear the table	clean your room	walk the dog
6	house	bungalow	apartment	kitchen

Understand the main ideas

1 a Match the types of homes to the photos.

1 apartment ......
2 houseboat ......
3 bungalow ......
4 castle ......
5 tree house ......
6 apartment block ......

a

b

c

d

e

f

b Choose the type of home you would like to live in.

2 a Read the text below and circle all the words and phrases about chores.

b Choose the correct answer (*a*, *b*, or *c*).

The text is about …

a how to organize household chores with a large family.
b a family doing household chores on a houseboat.
c family life in the Caribbean.

3 a Read the text again. Decide if the sentences are correct (*C*) or incorrect (*I*).

1 The Thompsons live on a canal in Cambridge. *I*
2 The houseboat is large and spacious. ......
3 Toby and Rob help with the household chores. ......
4 Josh is clearing the table. ......
5 Linda is the boys' cousin. ......
6 It's important to be organized and keep the houseboat clean. ......
7 Saturday is usually cleaning day for the Thompson family. ......
8 The boys like doing the ironing. ......

b Rewrite the incorrect sentences so that they are correct.

....
....
....
....
....

4 Match the underlined words in the texts with their opposites.

1 large *small*
2 boring ......
3 difficult ......
4 ugly ......
5 similar ......
6 relaxed ......

MOVE BEYOND

Look online for a video or story of people around the world who live in strange houses, for example, a tree house or a castle. How are their lives different from yours? Write three differences.

....
....
....

LIFE ON A HOUSEBOAT

It's 10:00 a.m. on a sunny Saturday morning on a houseboat on one of the many beautiful islands in the Caribbean. The Thompson family is busy doing household chores. The Thompson boys, Toby and Rob, are sorting the recycling and taking out the trash. There isn't a lot of space on the boat, so the whole family needs to be really organized! Sue, their mother, is hanging up the laundry while her husband, Josh, is making the beds. Today Linda, a family friend, is visiting. She's also helping with the household chores. She's in the kitchen clearing the table. As Toby explains, living on a houseboat isn't easy!

"Life on a houseboat is fun, but it's also a lot of work! We don't have much space, so we have to be neat. Saturday is always cleaning day on our houseboat, and things can get pretty crazy around here! When my brother and I are vacuuming or mopping the floor, and Mom and Dad are doing the laundry or loading the dishwasher, there's hardly any room to move!"

His brother, Rob, adds: *"Life on a houseboat is different and exciting, but living in a small space means keeping things neat! My brother and I don't like cleaning our room, and we argue about doing the ironing, but we know we have to help! When we finish our chores, we love going out with our friends. We usually swim in the ocean or look for pretty shells on the beach."*

GRAMMAR 1 Present progressive and simple present

Talk about things happening now and about habits and routines

1 Complete the grammar tables with the correct forms.

Present progressive

Affirmative		
I	am ('m)	helping my mom.
You/We/ (1)	are ('re)	washing the dishes. clearing the table.
He/She	(2) .... ('s)	(3) .... the ironing. making the bed.

Negative		
I	am ('m) not	taking out the trash.
You/We/ (4)	are not (aren't)	(5) .... the recycling. clearing the table.
He/She	(6) .... not (isn't)	loading the dishwasher. taking out the trash.

2 Complete the questions. Use Exercise 1 to help you.

Yes/No questions and short answers			
(1) .... you	watching	television?	(2) .... , I am. No, I'm not.
Is (3) .... / she	(4)	the table?	Yes, he/she (5) .... (6) .... , he/she isn't.

Wh- questions	
What are you (7) .... ?	(8) .... cleaning my room.
What (9) .... he/she doing?	He/She's (10) .... TV.

**3 Choose the correct tense to describe these situations (1–6).
Write *PP* (present progressive) or *SP* (simple present).**

1 for habits and routines ....
2 for actions that are happening now ....
3 for things that are generally true ....
4 for actions that are happening around now ....
5 with *never* and *rarely* ....
6 with (*right*) *now* and *today* ....

4 Underline the simple present and circle the present progressive verbs. Match each one to the uses (1–6) in Exercise 3.

19:30

JOSEPH: Hey Emma. What (are) you (doing)?
EMMA: Hi Joseph, right now I'm listening to music and surfing the net.
JOSEPH: Are you doing your homework?
EMMA: No ... I never <u>do</u> my homework before dinner.
JOSEPH: Wow! I'm too tired to do it after dinner!
EMMA: What are you doing tonight?
JOSEPH: Nothing interesting! Right now I'm studying for our chemistry test tomorrow. Chemistry is so hard.
EMMA: You're such a good student, Joseph!
JOSEPH: Are you going to the gym tonight?
EMMA: Sorry, I can't. I go to the gym on Saturday mornings, usually at 8:30 a.m.
JOSEPH: Oh, OK. I'm rarely awake then!

5 › Complete the sentences with the present progressive form of the verb in parentheses.

1 Right now, *I'm listening* (listen) to music on the bus.
2 The woman next to me on the bus ________ (read) a book.
3 There are two babies on the bus. They ________ (not / make) a lot of noise.
4 A boy ________ (ride) his bike next to the bus.
5 There's a man in the park. He ________ (not / play) the violin.
6 The man in the park ________ (play) the guitar.

6 › Choose the correct option to complete the sentences.

1 On weekends I normally (have) / *am having* breakfast at 9:00 a.m.
2 ***Do you sometimes help*** / ***Are you sometimes helping*** with the household chores?
3 It's 7:00 a.m. and Mia ***does*** / ***is doing*** the laundry.
4 We always ***swim*** / ***are swimming*** on Tuesdays.
5 Right now Farah is in town. She ***shops*** / ***is shopping*** with her cousin.
6 Ben and Alex are in the kitchen. They ***load*** / ***are loading*** the dishwasher.

7 ›› Complete the email with the correct options.

	a	b	c
1	a have	(b) am having	c has
2	a wake up	b is waking up	c are waking up
3	a are having	b has	c have
4	a am making	b make	c makes
5	a clean	b are cleaning	c am cleaning
6	a am liking	b like	c likes

Dear Raul,

I (1) *b* a great time here at my aunt's house in Toronto. Every morning we (2) ___ early and (3) ___ breakfast at home. Today is my aunt's birthday. I (4) ___ her a cake right now, and as a surprise, I (5) ___ the house! My aunt is great, and I (6) ___ her a lot.

Time to check on my cake!

See you soon,
Amy

8 ›› Complete the sentences using the correct stative verb in the box.

don't know   don't understand
hate   like   need   ~~want~~

1 I *want* to get a good grade on the French test, so I need to study a lot!
2 I ________ this TV show. It's funny.
3 Right now I ________ what to do this weekend.
4 Can you repeat that, please? I ________ what you're saying.
5 We have a special dinner tonight! We ________ to be at the restaurant at 6:00 p.m.
6 I ________ doing the ironing! It's so boring! Can you help me, please?

9 ››› Complete the conversation with the correct form of the verb in parentheses.

Amina: Hello?
Ben: Hey Amina, it's Ben.
Amina: Ben? It's 6:00 a.m.!
Ben: What (1) *are you doing* (you / do)?
Amina: I (2) ________ (sleep), of course. (3) ________ (you / wake up / always) this early?
Ben: Well, (4) ________ (I / not get up / always) early, but today (5) ________ (I / study) for my math test before school.
Amina: (6) ________ (you / read) your math textbook right now?
Ben: Yeah! (7) ________ (my brother / be) awake too. (8) ________ (he / make) breakfast.
Amina: You guys are crazy! (9) ________ (I / go) back to sleep now!

10 ››› Write questions for the answers.

1 Q: *What are you doing?*
A: I'm having breakfast and getting ready for school.
2 Q: ________
A: We normally have breakfast at 7:30 on school days.
3 Q: ________
A: They usually do their homework after school.
4 Q: ________
A: He's clearing the table and loading the dishwasher.
5 Q: *How often* ________
A: Jake gets up early every morning.
6 Q: ________
A: No, she's not sorting the recycling. She's taking out the trash.

LISTENING

Understand a situation

1 **Underline eight free-time activities and sports in the text.**

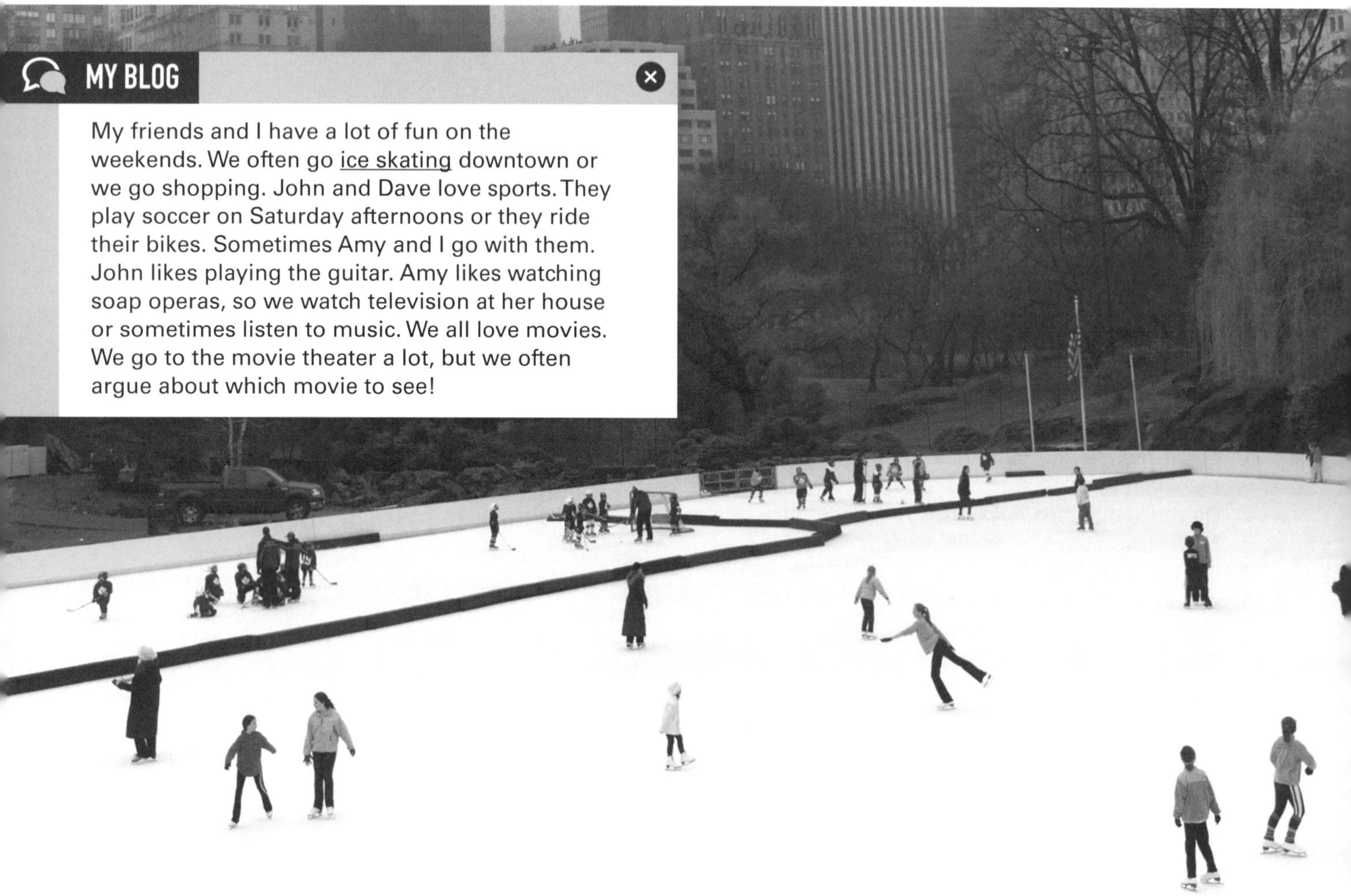

MY BLOG

My friends and I have a lot of fun on the weekends. We often go ice skating downtown or we go shopping. John and Dave love sports. They play soccer on Saturday afternoons or they ride their bikes. Sometimes Amy and I go with them. John likes playing the guitar. Amy likes watching soap operas, so we watch television at her house or sometimes listen to music. We all love movies. We go to the movie theater a lot, but we often argue about which movie to see!

2 ▶74 **Listen to the conversation and answer the questions.**

1 How many people are there? ....

2 Do they all know each other? ....

3 ▶74 **Listen again and write the names and activities you hear.**

1 Names: ...., ..., ...

2 Activities: ...., ..., ...

4 ▶74 **Listen again. Decide if the statements are correct (*C*) or incorrect (*I*). Rewrite the incorrect statements to make them correct.**

1 Carl and Anna are friends. ....

2 Carl and Josh are friends. ....

3 Josh is going to the movies. ....

4 Carl plays the saxophone. ....

5 Carl's class ends at 7:00. ....

6 Everyone likes ice skating. ....

5 ▶74 **Listen again. Who's speaking? Write Carl (*C*), Anna (*A*), or Josh (*J*).**

1 Hi Carl! Great to see you! ☐

2 This is my friend Josh. ☐

3 Nice to meet you! ☐

4 What's up, Carl? ☐

5 What are you doing later? ☐

6 See you there. ☐

Free-time activities

1 Complete the words. Rearrange the gray letters to find the mystery object.

1 Read a b o o k

2 Ride a _ _ _ _

3 Meet _ _ _ _ _ _ _

4 Go ice _ _ _ _ _ _ _

5 Watch _ _ _ _ _ _ _ _ _ _

6 _ _ _ _ _ _ to music

Mystery object: helmet

2 Write the words in the correct circle.

a book a magazine a text message ~~an instrument~~
soccer ice skating shopping tennis to the movies

play	go	read
an instrument		

3 a Choose the correct option to complete the sentences.

1 Listen to me play ***basketball*** / ***the piano***! I practice every day.
2 Alex is watching his favorite team play ***soccer*** / ***tennis*** on Saturday.
3 I'm reading a ***magazine*** / ***text message*** from Amy – she's coming right now.
4 We're going ***shopping*** / ***to the movies*** because I need a new shirt.
5 Are you reading the new ***text message*** / ***book*** by J. K. Rowling?
6 They're not going ***ice skating*** / ***to the movies*** with us because they don't like sad movies.

b Add an activity you like to each circle in Exercise 2.

WORDS & BEYOND

Choose the correct option to complete the sentences.

1 Where's the ***remote control*** / ***phone***? I want to change the channel.
2 I sometimes ***argue*** / ***go*** with my sister about our household chores.
3 My aunt loves the ***soap opera*** / ***song*** on TV right now. She watches it every week.
4 My brother's room is always a ***mess*** / ***clean***. He hates cleaning it.
5 I need to ***learn*** / ***study*** for my history test tomorrow.
6 I have to ***feed*** / ***walk*** the fish after school.

GRAMMAR 2 Present progressive for future arrangements

Talk about arrangements in the future

1 › Choose the correct option to complete the sentences.

Talking about now
We're having breakfast right now. I'm watching TV (1) *now* / *next week*.
Talking about arrangements in the future
I'm having a guitar lesson tomorrow morning. They're playing tennis (2) *tomorrow* / *right now*.

2 › Choose the correct option to complete the sentences.

1 ***I'm going*** / ***I go*** swimming tonight.
2 I ***don't go*** / ***'m not going*** to my grandparents' house this summer.
3 Next year my sister ***is leaving*** / ***leaves*** home for college.
4 This Friday ***I'm going to*** / ***I go to*** my guitar lesson early.
5 Sssh! The play ***starts*** / ***is starting*** now.
6 Tomorrow they ***'re meeting*** / ***meet*** some friends in the park.

3 › Look at the list of expressions. Do you use them to talk about the present or arrangements in the future? Write *N* (now) or *FA* (future arrangements) next to each one.

1 on the weekend ......
2 next month ......
3 now ......
4 tonight ......
5 tomorrow ......
6 right now ......

4 ›› (75) Complete the conversation between Mario and Fiona about their plans. Then listen and check your answers.

Fiona: What (1) *are you doing* (**do**) tomorrow night? Do you want to go to the movies?
Mario: Sorry, I can't. I (2) .... (**meet**) some friends.
Fiona: Oh, that's too bad! I (3) .... (**go**) to the movies with Tony. We're going shopping after the movie. It's Marta's birthday and we (4) .... (**buy**) her a present.

Mario: I can meet my friends early. Then I can go shopping with you and Tony later!
Fiona: Perfect! Tony (5) .... (**come**) to the movie theater at 5:00 p.m. We can meet at 7:00 p.m. at the mall.
Mario: Sounds great! See you then!

5 ›› Decide if the sentences are correct (*C*) or incorrect (*I*).

1 Fiona's going to the movies tomorrow night. ......
2 Mario's going to the movies tomorrow night. ......
3 It's Marta's birthday today. ......
4 They're buying Marta a present. ......
5 Tony's meeting friends tomorrow night. ......
6 Mario's not going shopping with Fiona. ......

6 ››› Look at Jane's calendar and correct the sentences.

MONDAY	TUESDAY	WEDNESDAY
Study for math test	*Play tennis with Jo*	*Help Mom with household chores*
THURSDAY	**FRIDAY**	**SATURDAY & SUNDAY**
Movies with Marcos	*Ice skating with Judy*	*Visit grandparents*

1 She's going swimming on Tuesday.
She isn't going swimming on Tuesday.
She's playing tennis with Jo.
2 She's going to the movies with her mom on Thursday.
....
3 She's studying for her math test on Friday.
....
4 She's going ice skating on Tuesday.
....
5 She's helping her mom on Monday.
....
6 She's playing tennis with her mom on Tuesday.
....

7 a ››› Choose the correct option to complete the sentences.

1 Today is Monday. ***Tomorrow*** / ***Tonight*** is Tuesday.
2 It's Friday, July 4th. ***In two weeks' time*** / ***Next week*** it's going to be Friday, July 11th.
3 This morning I'm going to school, this afternoon I'm doing my homework, and ***tonight*** / ***this morning*** I'm going to the movies.
4 It's 2017. ***Next month*** / ***Next year***, in 2018, I'm starting middle school.
5 ***This weekend*** / ***This year***, on Saturday, I'm meeting my friends at the park.
6 It's four o'clock. I'm meeting my friends at nine o'clock ***tonight*** / ***on weekends*** to go shopping.

b Write three sentences about your future plans.

....
....
....

Check that you understand on the phone

1 Complete the phrases with the words in the box. Practice saying the phrases.

again from how this is message on repeat speak

1 Hello, can I ______ to Tony, please?
2 Hold ______ ...
3 Could you ______ that, please?
4 ______ do you spell that?
5 Can you say that ______ please?
6 Hello, ______ Tony.
7 I'm calling ______ Los Angeles.
8 Can I leave a ______ ?

2 Number the conversation in the correct order.

1 **Anna:** Hello, this is Anna.
__ **Anna:** I'm sorry, Tony isn't here right now.
__ **Maria:** Hello, it's Maria. Can I speak to Tony, please?
__ **Anna:** Yes, of course. Let me get a pen.
__ **Anna:** How do you spell that, please?
__ **Maria:** Please tell him we're meeting at 3:00 p.m. at the Unicorn Cafe.
__ **Maria:** Oh. Can I leave a message?
__ **Maria:** U-N-I-C-O-R-N.
__ **Maria:** Thanks a lot. Bye.
__ **Anna:** OK, got it.

3 Look at Exercise 2. What phrases do Anna and Maria use to ...

1 be polite?

______

2 explain the problem?

______

3 ask for more information?

______

4 76 Complete the conversation with the expressions below. Then listen and check your answers.

a Hold on
b Can you say that again, please?
c Can I help you?
d 733-8025
e What time are the classes?
f The 6:00 p.m. class is full.

Woman: Woodland Community Center. (1) c
Brad: Hello. I'm calling about swimming classes.
Woman: (2) __ ... There are swimming classes on Tuesdays and on Thursdays.
Brad: (3) __
Woman: At 3:00 p.m. or 6:00 p.m.
Brad: Can I sign up for the 6:00 p.m. class?
Woman: (4) __ You can leave your name and number if you want.
Brad: OK. My name's Brad Stinston.
Woman: (5) __ Simpson?
Brad: No, Stinston. S-T-I-N-S-T-O-N.
Woman: All right. What's your telephone number?
Brad: (6) __
Woman: Perfect. We're starting more classes in the summer.
Brad: Oh, OK. Thank you very much!

5 77 PRONOUNCE Listen and underline the silent letter(s) in each word. Then practice repeating the words.

autumn castle half island knee knife know listen sign walk Wednesday wrong

WRITING

Use *and*, *also*, and *too*

1 Choose the correct option to complete the sentences.

1 This afternoon Todd is playing tennis ***and*** / ***also*** soccer.
2 He's studying for his math test and helping his brother ***also*** / ***too***.
3 He plays tennis and he ***also*** / ***too*** plays the piano.
4 Todd likes listening to music ***too*** / ***and*** reading magazines.
5 Todd is going to the movies on Saturday night. His friend is ***also*** / ***too*** going.
6 Todd's brother's going to the museum. His cousins are going ***too*** / ***also***.

2 Complete the sentences with *and*, *also*, and *too*.

1 I like staying at my grandparents' house but I *also* like my apartment.
2 Our town has a beautiful castle. There's a museum ______ .
3 My brother likes listening to music ______ watching music videos.
4 I'm going shopping next week. My friends are coming ______ .
5 I'm cleaning the house, and I'm ______ listening to music.
6 I want to leave my name ______ my phone number.

3 Read the messages and fill in the blanks with *and*, *also*, or *too*.

MESSAGES

I'm at the sports center! I'm playing tennis with my sister, (1) ______ we're meeting friends later for a soccer game. What are you doing? You can come and play (2) ______ !

3:34 p.m.

MESSAGES

I'm sitting on the bus. I'm meeting my brother downtown in 10 minutes. He wants to buy a present for his girlfriend, (3) ______ I'm helping him! He's getting her some flowers (4) ______ . See you later.

6:00 p.m.

MESSAGES

I'm going to the National Museum of Modern Art on Sunday with my cousins. My brother's (5) ______ coming with his friend Dylan. Do you want to join us (6) ______ ?

10:00 a.m.

4 Write sentences using the prompts and the word in parentheses.

1 James / wash / dishes / ironing . (also)
James is washing the dishes. He's also doing the ironing.
2 We / study / math / French . (too)
______
3 I / be / tired / hungry . (and)
______
4 Alison / play / piano / violin . (also)
______
5 They / go / movies / museum . (too)
______
6 It / be / dark / cold . (and)
______

5 a Solve the code. Complete the instant messages.

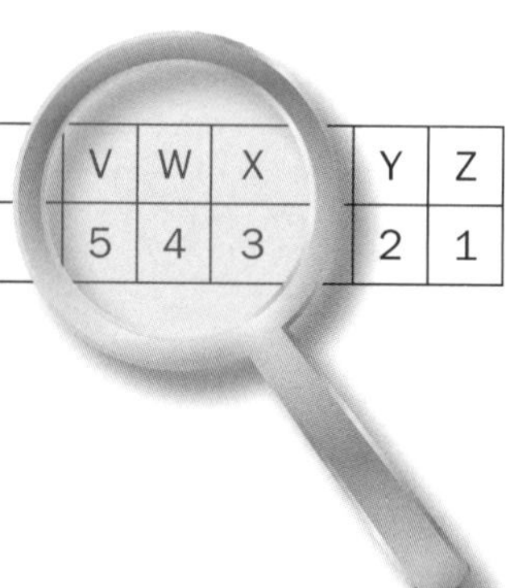

A	B	C	D	E	F	G	H	I	J	K	L	M	N	O	P	Q	R	S	T	U	V	W	X	Y	Z
26	25	24	23	22	21	20	19	18	17	16	15	14	13	12	11	10	9	8	7	6	5	4	3	2	1

W	H	E	R	E															?
4	19	22	9	22		26	9	22		2	12	6		20	12	18	13	20	

	'																	.
18		14		20	12	18	13	20		8	19	12	11	11	18	13	20	

b Use the code to write a message to a friend.

______
______

6 **Write three instant messages to a friend. Use the *Ideas box* and the *Writing plan* to help you prepare.**

IDEAS BOX

clean your room do the laundry do your homework go ice skating go shopping play tennis read a book watch television

WRITING PLAN

Make notes for each of your messages.

1 Write the time you're sending the message.
Message 1: ……
Message 2: ……
Message 3: ……

2 Describe what you're doing now.
Message 1: ……
Message 2: ……
Message 3: ……

3 Join similar ideas with *and*, *too*, and *also*.
Message 1: ……
Message 2: ……
Message 3: ……

4 Talk about your arrangements for later or for the weekend.
Message 1: ……
Message 2: ……
Message 3: ……

WRITE AND CHECK

7 **Write your messages. Check (✓) the stages in the plan.**

SEND

SEND

SEND

Identify the cause of a problem

GET THINKING

1 **Read Dave and Sam's points of view. Are these good solutions to their problems? Why or why not?**

Solution A: Dave could buy Sam a juice after swimming. ***good*** / ***bad*** solution
Solution B: Sam could give Dave back his Metallic Three CD. ***good*** / ***bad*** solution

Dave
It's not fair. He's my best friend, and he doesn't want to lend me the money for the Metallic Three *concert. He gets a bigger allowance than me anyway. And he still has my* Metallic Three *CD. In fact he still has three of my CDs. We always go to concerts together, so why can't he pay for my ticket? I can pay him back next month.*

Sam
I always buy him a carton of juice after swimming, but he never buys me a drink. When I lend him money, he never says when he can pay me back. I'm not allowed to go to the concert by myself, but I'm not paying for Dave.

2 **Answer the questions.**

1 What event are Dave and Sam unhappy about? ……
2 What else is Dave unhappy about? ……
3 What else is Sam unhappy about? ……

3 **Think of your own solutions to Dave and Sam's problems.**

……
……
……

1 Match the words to make compound nouns.

1 soap — a message
2 dining — b game
3 pencil — c console
4 app — d browser
5 text — e case
6 video — f store
7 web — g room
8 games — h opera

2 Complete sentences 1–10. Then check your answers by finding the words in the word search.

1 Do you have *brothers* and sisters?
2 I'm going ______ at the pool.
3 We're playing music on my new ______ .
4 She's listening to music on her ______ , so she can't hear you.
5 My dad is ______ the table for dinner.
6 My team ______ soccer on Sunday afternoons.
7 I ______ my teeth before I take a shower.
8 I love to eat, but I can't ______ !
9 My mom does the ______ at night.
10 You keep your clothes in a ______ .

b	w	a	c	l	o	s	e	t	i
r	x	s	w	i	m	m	i	n	g
o	e	p	h	e	c	a	r	w	l
t	r	l	t	b	r	c	o	o	k
h	e	a	d	p	h	o	n	e	s
e	r	y	p	f	x	o	i	x	v
r	j	s	g	k	m	l	n	q	z
s	b	r	u	s	h	e	g	y	u
o	m	p	3	p	l	a	y	e	r
m	s	e	t	t	i	n	g	p	i

3 Complete the table. Match the nouns in the box to the correct verbs.

a book   a computer   a magazine   a mouse   a movie   a printer   basketball   television   tennis

watch	play	read	use

4 Choose the correct option to complete the sentences.

1 We switch **off** / **on** all the lights when we go out. It saves electricity.
2 I go **on** / **out** with my friends every weekend.
3 I find it difficult to switch **off** / **on** at night. I need to relax more.
4 You need a password to log **on** / **off** to the website.
5 Can you please take **on** / **out** the trash before you go to school?
6 I need to find **out** / **on** more information about New York before I do my project.

ALL ABOUT ME

1 What household chores do you usually do?

______

2 Describe your bedroom.

In my bedroom there's a …
In my bedroom I have a …

______
______
______

1 Use the words to write questions. Then use the words in parentheses to write answers.

1 you / write email
Q: How often *do you write email* ?
A: I ______ (sometimes)
2 he / update his blog
Q: How often ______ ?
A: He ______ (from time to time)
3 your mom / send text messages
Q: How often ______ ?
A: She ______ (not regularly)
4 Teo and Raul / download apps
Q: How often ______ ?
A: They ______ (always)
5 she / use her laptop for homework
Q: How often ______ ?
A: She ______ (hardly ever)

2 Choose the correct options to complete the text.

It's 8:30 a.m. at the school playground. School (1) ***start*** / ***starts*** at 9:00 a.m. A lot of students are waiting outside. Some students (2) ***are listening*** / ***listen*** to music and others (3) ***are talking*** / ***talk*** to their friends. Normally many of the boys (4) ***are playing*** / ***play*** soccer before school, but today nobody (5) ***'s playing*** / ***plays*** because they have exams. A few students (6) ***are reading*** / ***read*** their notebooks and (7) ***studying*** / ***study*** for their exam in the afternoon. Most students (8) ***don't like*** / ***aren't liking*** exams, so they look very nervous.

3 Choose the correct options from the box below to complete the text.

My family and I live on (1) *c* houseboat in Kamloops, Canada. (2) ___ two bedrooms, a bathroom, and a very small kitchen on the boat. We have everything we (3) ___ on the houseboat, and it's an exciting way of life! My sister and I sometimes (4) ___ about who is responsible for (5) ___ household chores, but we (6) ___ get along well. Right now from my bedroom on the boat I (7) ___ the Rocky Mountains! I like (8) ___ on our houseboat!

1	a the	b an	c a	d some
2	a We're	b There's	c It's in	d There are
3	a needing	b are needing	c need	d needs
4	a arguing	b argue	c am arguing	d are arguing
5	a a	b the	c an	d this
6	a never	b always	c are usually	d usually
7	a sees	b am seeing	c seeing	d can see
8	a live	b living	c lives	d to live

4 Complete the conversation with the correct form of the verb in parentheses.

Hi Mary, it's Todd.

Oh, hi Todd. What's up?

What (1) are you doing *(do) this weekend?*

On Saturday morning I'm helping my parents with the household chores. I always (2) ______ (clean) my room and (3) ______ (vacuum) the living room on Saturdays. I (4) ______ usually ______ (do) my homework until Sunday afternoon.

Oh, OK ...

On Saturday afternoon I (5) ______ (meet) my friends. We (6) ______ (go) shopping together and to the movies too! Do you want to come?

Um, no thanks. I don't like shopping. My mom and sister (7) ______ (shop) right now, but I'm reading! What (8) ______ (do) on Sunday?

On Sunday morning my dad (9) ______ (take) me to the Science Museum. Then I need to do my homework!

Wow! Busy weekend.

What are you doing this weekend, Todd?

Nothing special! That's why I (10) ______ (call) you!

5 Rearrange the words to make sentences. Use the correct form of the verb.

1 Paco / go / to the movies / hardly ever .
Paco hardly ever goes to the movies.
2 the ironing / do / Maria / now .
______
3 make / for lunch / pizza / Mom / today .
______
4 my bed / make / I / every morning .
______
5 fly / to New York / My dad / on Friday night .
______
6 study / I / Tonight / for my exams / my homework / and / do .
______

WILD WORLD

VOCABULARY 1 >>> Landscapes and natural features

1 Label the features on the map.

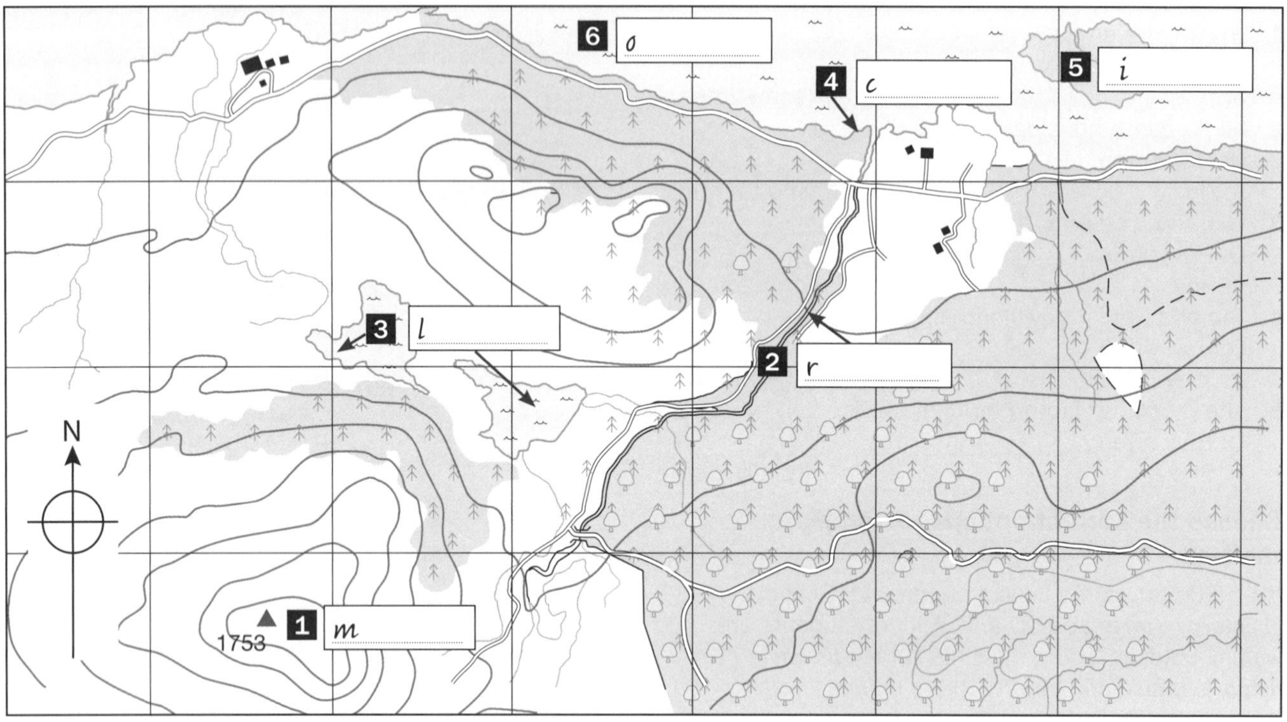

2 a Write the words in the correct circles.

beach ~~coast~~ countryside desert flower grass hill island lake mountain ocean river savannah stream tree

water

land
coast

plants

b Add one more natural feature to each circle.

3 a Complete the sentences with the words in the box.

beach countryside desert forest ice sheet savannah stream

1 There's some sand or small stones, and it's next to the ocean. ....
2 There's a lot of sand and almost no water. ....
3 It's a small river. ....
4 There are fields, flowers, and trees. ....
5 It has a lot of grass and it's very flat. ....
6 It's very cold. You can find it in the Antarctic. ....
7 There are a lot of trees. ....

b Choose one of the places to visit. Give two reasons why.

....

....

4 Choose the best options to complete the postcard.

Hi Katie!

We're having a great time in this little town on the (1) **coast / desert** of Uruguay. The town is beside a river. Sometimes we go for a walk in the (2) **hills / lake** behind the town. There's a beautiful forest with a lot of (3) **islands / trees** and (4) **flowers / ice**. Sometimes we go down to the (5) **beach / stream** and play volleyball on the sand and go swimming in the (6) **ocean / desert**. The water is warm!

See you soon!
Ian

READING

Find specific information

1 Choose the correct option to complete the sentences.

REMEMBER HOW TO ...

find specific information

- Don't read (1) ***all*** / ***most*** of the text.
- Read the (2) ***end*** / ***beginning*** of each paragraph. Does it have the information you need? If not, read the (3) ***first*** / ***next*** paragraph.
- Look for words connected to the (4) ***paragraphs*** / ***information*** you need.

2 Look at the title of the article and the picture. What do you think the article is about? Choose two answers.

a watching lions
b using lights
c saving lions
d planting trees

3 Read the article quickly. Which paragraph answers each question?

1 Where is the boy from? 2
2 Where did the cows stay at night? ......
3 What problem did Richard try to solve? ......
4 Why is it a problem to kill lions? ......
5 What made him think of a solution? ......
6 How did he solve the problem on his farm? ......

LIGHTS TO SAVE LIONS

1 **Richard Turere is 13 years old. In 2012, he made a speech at the TED® conference in California. TED (Technology, Entertainment, and Design) is a conference for people from all over the world. What did Richard talk about?**

2 Richard was born in Kenya, near Nairobi National Park. When he was nine years old, he started taking care of his father's cattle. At night, the cows went into a small shed.

3 The problem was that lions came out at night. They often killed the cows and ate them. So the farmers killed the lions. That was also a problem because lions are one of the biggest tourist attractions in Kenya, especially in Nairobi National Park. In the past, there were over half a million lions, but now there are only about 2,000 lions still alive in Kenya.

4 Richard tried to think of a way to protect the cows. When he went out at night, he used a flashlight. He noticed that lions are afraid of moving lights. Using some broken parts from motorcycle lights and a solar panel, he made lights that flashed on and off around the cattle shed.

5 His idea was successful and he installed lights for his neighbors too. His idea saved the cattle and saved the lions too.

4 Read the article again. Choose the correct answer.

1 What did the boy do?
   a He's 13 years old.
   b He killed a lion.
   c He made a speech.
2 Where is the boy from?
   a He was born in Kenya.
   b He looked after his father's cattle.
   c The cows went into a small shed.
3 What problem did he try to solve?
   a There were too many lions.
   b Lions often killed the cows and ate them.
   c Lions were a tourist attraction.
4 Why is it a problem to kill lions?
   a The farmers need them.
   b There are half a million lions.
   c There are only 2,000 lions left in Kenya.
5 What did he notice that made him think of a solution?
   a Farmers kill lions.
   b Lions come out at night.
   c Lions are afraid of moving lights.
6 How did he solve the problem?
   a He stayed with the cattle every night.
   b He made lights that flashed on and off.
   c His idea was successful.

5 Look at the article again and find ...

1 the name of a country. ......
2 the name of a conference. ......
3 the names of two kinds of animals. ....
4 a place to keep cattle. ......
5 the name of a tourist attraction. ......
6 the names of two types of equipment. ....

6 Why was Richard's idea special? Choose the correct option to complete the sentences.

1 He ***needed*** / ***didn't need*** a lot of materials.
2 His idea ***was*** / ***wasn't*** expensive.
3 He ***helped*** / ***didn't help*** the farmers.
4 The lions ***stopped*** / ***started*** eating the cows.
5 The farmers ***killed*** / ***didn't kill*** the lions.
6 Richard ***saved*** / ***didn't save*** the lions and the cows.

MOVE BEYOND

Use the internet to find out three more facts about Richard Turere.

1 ......
2 ......
3 ......

GRAMMAR 1 Simple past

Describe completed events in the past

1 Complete the grammar table with the correct forms.

Simple past *wh-* questions				Answers
When	(1) ______	they	start school?	When they (2) ______ five.
What	(3) ______	he	say to her?	He (4) ______ yes.
Why	(5) ______	you	do your homework?	I forgot, sorry.
What	(6) ______	the	right answers?	I don't know.
What	(7) ______	their	names?	Paul and Toby.
How	(8) ______	his	cooking?	It was good!
How	(9) ______	her	parents?	They (10) ______ nice.
Simple past *yes/no* questions				**Answers**
Did	(11) ______	win	the competition?	Yes, she did.
Didn't	they	go	to school today?	No, they (12) ______ .
Were	you	invited	to the party?	Yes, I (13) ______ .
Was	she	happy	with her present?	No, she (14) ______ .

2 Write the verbs and their past forms in the table.

~~be~~ come do go ~~help~~ like start stop study teach travel win

Regular verbs		Irregular verbs	
help	*helped*	*be*	*was/were*

3 Choose the correct option to complete the grammar rules.

1 Use the simple past to talk about ___ in the past.
  a completed actions
  b unfinished actions

2 To form the simple past, add ___ to the verb.
  a *-ed*
  b *-es*

3 Use ___ to form *yes/no* questions in the past with most verbs.
  a *do*
  b *did*

4 Use *did* + ___ to form negatives.
  a *no*
  b *not*

4 Complete the questions with a question word from the box and *did/didn't*.

how what when where why (x2)

1 ______ you do last night?

2 ______ they feel after the exam?

3 ______ Sarah leave the party? Before 11:00 p.m.?

4 ______ she grow up? In Boston?

5 ______ you ask Tom to come to the party? I thought he was your friend.

6 ______ you come? You missed all the fun.

5 › **Complete the sentences with the simple past form of the verb in parentheses.**

1 We __________ (do) a survey about ways to save energy.
2 They __________ (start) a campaign to plant trees.
3 We __________ (clean) up the local beach.
4 Our team __________ (win) a prize for Young Environmental Ideas of the Year.
5 She __________ (speak) at a conference.
6 We __________ (make) a website for our campaign.

6 ›› **Complete the conversation with the verbs in the box. Use the simple past.**

be (x2) do (x3) not expect explain give make not reply start stop win write

Sue: (1) __________ your class __________ an environment prize?
Becky: Yes, we (2) __________ . We (3) __________ to win – it's amazing!
Sue: Congratulations! What (4) __________ your project about?
Becky: We (5) __________ a campaign for green products. We (6) __________ presentations at different schools. We (7) __________ about reading labels and finding out what's in our food and clothes and things we buy.
Sue: (8) __________ the students interested in the campaign?
Becky: Oh yes! They (9) __________ letters and email to supermarkets and department stores.
Sue: (10) __________ it __________ a difference?
Becky: Well, you know, they (11) __________ at most stores, but some stores (12) __________ selling products with chemicals in them.
Sue: That's so cool!
Becky: I know.

7 ›› **Find and correct the mistakes. Use the simple past.**

1 They start the project last year.
____
2 They saw a movie about Thailand before they leave.
____
3 She decide to started a campaign.
____
4 We aren't know about the wildlife problems there.
____
5 What they did discover about the environment?
____
6 They didn't were nervous about their talk.
____
7 Did you traveled to the USA?
____
8 Did you gave a presentation at another school?
____

8 a ››› **Make questions using the prompts. Use the simple past.**

1 What / Richard / invent?
____
2 What / the problem?
____
3 he / successful?
____
4 How / he / save the lions?
____
5 he / save the cattle?
____

b ››› **Look at the Reading text on page 33. In your notebook, answer the questions from Exercise 8a using the simple past.**

LISTENING

Take notes

1 Complete the tips with the words in the box.

REMEMBER HOW TO …

take notes

great	horrible	important	spelling	symbols

- Only write the most (1) ________ words or ideas.
- Use (2) ________ . For example: ☺ for (3) ________ /*fantastic*, ☹ for (4) ________ , & for *and*.
- Don't worry about (5) ________ and grammar. You can check these later.

2 a Rewrite the following sentences in note form.

1 The bear was very big. We were scared!

____

2 We saw a lot of elephants – about five I think. It was great!

____

3 She really doesn't like snakes after she had a bad experience on vacation.

____

b Look at the animals in the photos. Which words in the box do you connect with them?

desert	forest	ice	ocean	river	savannah

a 

b 

c 

3 ▶78 Listen to three conversations and complete the notes.

Q: What's your most interesting animal experience?

		What did the animals do?
1 ☺ or ☹	________	a came into the hotel
When?	________	b came into the garden
Where?	________	c came up to the window
Which animal?	________	
2 ☺ or ☹	________	**What did the animals do?**
When?	________	a took my camera
Where?	________	b attacked us
Which animal?	________	c chased us
3 ☺ or ☹	________	**What did the animals do?**
When?	________	a came into the garden
Where?	________	b came into our tent
Which animal?	________	c came into our kitchen

4 ▶78 Listen again and answer these questions.

Conversation 1

1 How many animals were in the group?

____

2 How long do these animals live?

____

Conversation 2

3 What do these animals eat?

____

4 What do these animals do in the winter?

____

Conversation 3

5 How many of these animals are there in Florida?

____

6 Why is the population increasing?

____

VOCABULARY 2

Wildlife

1 Match the animals (1–6) to the descriptions (a–f) below. Write the name of each animal.

1 ....

2 ....

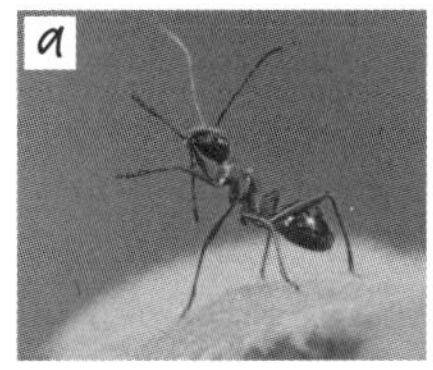

3 *ant*

4 ....

5 ....

6 ....

a They live in large groups. They work very hard. They have six legs.
b They have big eyes. They eat mice and small rabbits. They fly at night.
c They eat frogs. They're long and thin. They can live on land or in water.
d They have bright colors. They sometimes talk. They can fly.
e They walk on two feet. They can swim. They live in the Antarctic.
f They swim in small groups. They can talk to each other. They live in the ocean.

2 Choose the correct option to complete the facts below. You may need help with this.

ANIMAL QUIZ

1 Spiders have ____ legs.
a six **b** eight **c** ten

2 Turtles lay their eggs ____ .
a in the ocean
b on land
c in trees

3 Polar bears live in ____ .
a France **b** Alaska
c China

4 Frogs usually eat ____ .
a insects **b** fruit
c plants

5 Bees have ____ eyes.
a two **b** three **c** five

6 Crocodiles usually lay ____ eggs at one time.
a 2–3 **b** 20–30 **c** 30–50

3 Rearrange the letters to find the names of animals. Match them to the descriptions. There's more than one answer for some animals.

1	wol *owl*	a	It's a reptile.
2	psdrie	b	It eats other animals.
3	eeb	c	It has eight legs.
4	rbae	d	It's an insect.
5	utrlet	e	It can fly.
6	ecrilroocd	f	It lives in water.

WORDS & BEYOND

Choose the correct option to complete the sentences.

1 Let's start a ***campaign*** / ***goal*** to save dolphins.
2 Let's ***plant*** / ***join*** a tree to help stop climate change.
3 Let's ***talk*** / ***make*** a speech about animals.
4 Let's ***pick up*** / ***save*** litter in the park.
5 Let's ***do*** / ***take part*** in a wildlife campaign.
6 Let's help them to ***raise*** / ***reach*** their goals.

GRAMMAR 2 Past progressive and simple past

Talk about actions in progress and finished actions in the past

1 › Complete the grammar tables with the correct forms.

Past progressive – affirmative statements			
You, We, They	(1) ________	watching	TV.
I, She, He, It	was	eating	breakfast.
Past progressive – negative statements			
You, We, They	weren't	playing	soccer.
I, She, He, It	(2) ________	writing	a postcard.

Past progressive – *wh-* questions				Answers
What	(3) ________	you, we, they	doing?	I (4) ________ sleeping.
	(5) ________	she, he, it, I		She (6) ________ sleeping.
Past progressive – *yes/no* questions				**Answers**
Were	you, we, they	swimming	in the pool?	Yes, we (7) ________ .
Was	she, he, it, I			No, she (8) ________ .

2 › Write the *-ing* form of each verb.

verb	*-ing* form
play	*playing*
get	
visit	
stop	
travel	
sleep	
write	
swim	

3 ›› Choose the correct option to complete the rules.

1 Use the past progressive for actions ____ at a particular time in the past.
  a in progress b completed
2 Make the past progressive with ____ and verb + *-ing*.
  a *is/are* b *was/were*
3 Don't use the past progressive with verbs like ____ .
  a *go* and *live* b *know* and *believe*

4 ›› Complete the sentences with the past progressive.

1 What ________ (you all / do) at 5:00 p.m. yesterday?
2 ________ (I / wait) for a bus.
3 ________ (Sharon / not ride) her bike last night.
4 ________ (Sam and Andy / swim) in the lake.
5 "________ (they / visit) their friends?"
"Yes, they were."
6 ________ (we / not talk), but we still didn't hear the bell.

5 ››› Complete the conversations with the simple past or past progressive.

1 **A:** ________ (Robbie / ride) his bike this morning?
B: No, ________ (he / be). ________ (he / play) soccer with his friends. Why?
A: ________ (I / call) him and there was no answer!

2 **A:** ________ (we / see) you in the car yesterday with your mom. Where ________ (you / go)?
B: Oh yes! ________ (we / take) our cat to the vet yesterday. It's sick.

3 **A:** What ________ (you / do) yesterday morning at 9:00 a.m.? ________ (you / sleep)?
B: No, ________ (I / be)! ________ (Cara and I / make) breakfast for the family.

6 ››› Complete the story with the simple past or the past progressive.

Last year I went camping in Canada. I (1) ________ (take) this picture while we (2) ________ (climb) in the Rockies. One night I (3) ________ (hear) a strange noise while we (4) ________ (put) up the tent. I (5) ________ (not know) that a bear (6) ________ (follow) us. I (7) ________ (turn) on the flashlight and (8) ________ (see) the bear. It (9) ________ (wait) behind a tree. I (10) ________ (shout) for help and the bear (11) ________ (run) away.

SPEAKING

Make and react to suggestions

1 a ▶79 **Some students are thinking of ways to improve the environment. Listen to the conversation and check (✓) the ideas that are mentioned.**

Ways to Go Green

- Start a school Recycling Campaign. ☐
- Raise money for your local animal shelter. ☐
- Persuade everyone to go "veggie" once a week. ☐
- Have a No Plastic Bottle Day. ☐
- Wear only organic materials. ☐
- Promote (tell people about) recycled paper products. ☐
- Organize a local park clean-up day. ☐

b Which idea do they choose?

2 ▶79 **Listen again and check (✓) the phrases you hear. Practice repeating them.**

Make suggestions
- ☐ What should we do … ?
- ☐ What could we … ?
- ☐ We could …
- ☐ Let's …
- ☐ Why don't we … ?
- ☐ How about … ?

React to suggestions
- ☐ No way!
- ☐ I don't know.
- ☐ That's pretty serious.
- ☐ That's not very exciting.
- ☐ That's a nice idea.

3 Match the sentence parts to make suggestions.

1	Let's	a	wear for the school Green Day?
2	How about	b	could have a No Plastic Bottle Day.
3	Why don't	c	we raise money for a charity?
4	What should	d	start a recycling program.
5	We	e	a Green Clothing Day?
6	What could we	f	we do for our project?

4 a Number the conversation in the correct order.

____ **Andy:** OK. Let's think of a good logo for the poster.
____ **Andy:** I'm making a poster for the school Green Day. Do you have any ideas?
____ **Andy:** That's a nice idea! Everyone can walk or ride a bike to school.
____ **Martin:** That's right, or they can take a bus.
_1_ **Martin:** What are you doing?
____ **Martin:** Yes! Why don't we organize a Car-free Day.

b Think about ways to help the environment. Think of three things you do now and three things you want to do.

....
....
....
....
....
....

5 ▶80 PRONOUNCE **Listen and find the verb in each group that has an /ɔ/ sound. Practice repeating the words.**

1	started	walked	got
2	taught	won	told
3	stopped	thought	was
4	said	began	saw

WRITING

Write a story with time expressions

a

b

c

d

1 Write one sentence about each picture. Use the simple past or past progressive.

a ....

b ....

c ....

d ....

2 a Choose the correct options to complete the story. Then number the sections in the correct order (1–4).

The dog and the rabbit

____ a (1) **Yesterday** / **Then** the dog turned around and ... the rabbit was sitting on the dog's back! The dog was bringing the rabbit safely back! I took a picture and (2) **later** / **yesterday** I showed it to my dad. He thought it was terrific!

_1_ b Something really funny happened (3) **yesterday** / **after** morning. I was walking in the park near the lake when I saw a dog. At first it was running along very happily, but a few minutes (4) **then** / **later** it started barking loudly.

____ c The dog was chasing a rabbit. The rabbit ran into the lake and started swimming.

____ d (5) **Then** / **After** the dog jumped into the lake and swam after the rabbit. (6) **Later** / **After** a few minutes the dog caught the rabbit, and I was really worried about it.

b Look at the pictures again and number them in the correct order.

3 Look at the completed story in Exercise 2 again. Match the parts of the story to the sentences.

1 The introduction
2 The first event
3 The second event
4 The third event
5 The conclusion

a The dog was chasing a rabbit.
b I showed a photo to my dad.
c I was walking in the park.
d The dog brought the rabbit back.
e The rabbit and the dog ran into the lake.

4 Choose the correct option to complete the sentences.

1 How ***did*** / ***was*** the rabbit feel?
2 Why ***was*** / ***did*** the dog go into the lake?
3 ***Did*** / ***Was*** the rabbit escape?
4 The dog ***wasn't*** / ***didn't*** hurt the rabbit.
5 The rabbit ***wasn't*** / ***didn't*** afraid.
6 ***Was*** / ***Did*** the boy happy?

5 Complete the sentences with the time expressions in the box.

at first	during the night	last night	later	then

1 .... I had a very strange experience.
2 It happened .... when everyone else was asleep.
3 I woke up because it was so light outside. .... I woke my brother up to show him.
4 .... he was scared – he thought it was aliens!
5 .... he was more relaxed. "It's probably the full moon," he said. In the end we laughed because he was right.

6 **You are going to write a story. Order your ideas in a plan. Use the *Writing plan* to help you prepare.**

WRITING PLAN

Make notes for your answer.

1 Introduction: Think of or imagine a funny story about an animal.
When did it happen? ....
Where did it happen? ....
What were you doing? ....

2 Describe exactly what happened. What happened first? What happened next? How did the story end?
Event 1 ....
Event 2 ....
Event 3 ....

3 Say how you felt. Was it funny/scary/exciting? Think of a conclusion.
....
....

4 Add some time expressions to your answers above. Look at the box for ideas.

Time expressions
At first ... Later ... A few minutes later ...
After a while ... After a short time ...

WRITE AND CHECK

7 **Write your story. Check (✓) the stages in the plan.**

Use mind maps to organize information for a talk

1 **Look at Anya's mind map. Why did she make it? Check (✓) the correct reason.**
- to help her learn vocabulary
- to organize ideas for a new project
- to organize her notes from a class

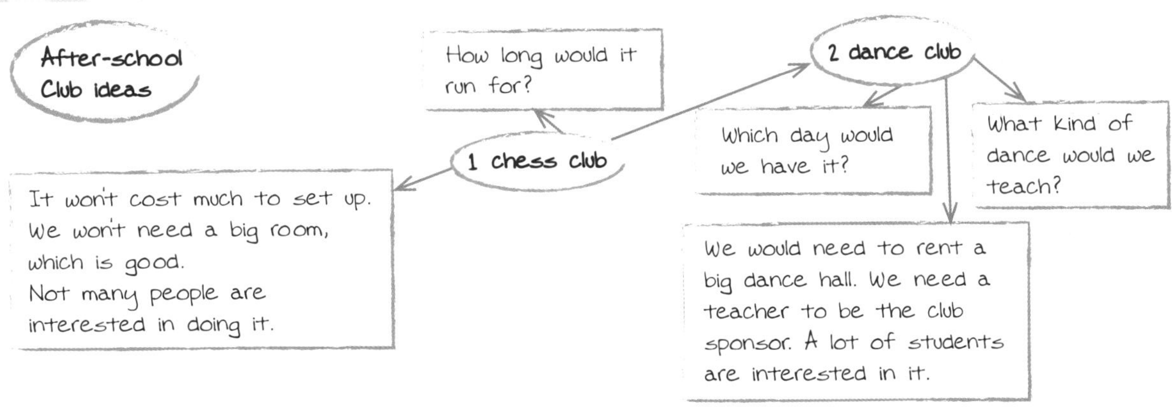

2 **Look at the tips for making a mind map. Check (✓) the ones that Anya used in her map.**
- Start with a main word or idea.
- Draw lines from the words and pictures.
- Write one or two key words on each line.
- Use CAPITAL LETTERS for important words.
- Group similar information in boxes.

3 **Look at the notes (in boxes) in Anya's mind map and decide if they are advantages (☺), disadvantages, (☹) or questions (?).**

4 **In your notebook reorganize Anya's mind map. Add headings and use your own words to summarize the information.**

1 Find the odd word out in each group. Write down why it's different.

1	tablet	calculator	laptop	(map)
	It's not an electronic device.			
2	mouse	cell phone	keyboard	monitor
3	kettle	bed	table	chair
4	dishwasher	washing machine	refrigerator	bed
5	skating	tennis	shopping	swimming
6	beach	forest	hill	bear
7	penguin	dolphin	turtle	mountain
8	cousin	brother	grandfather	uncle
9	turtle	snake	crocodile	ant
10	pencil case	notebook	house key	school bag

2 Choose the best option to complete the quiz.

1 ____ live in the desert.
a Owls b Snakes c Parrots

2 ____ live on the savannah.
a Bears b Elephants
c Turtles

3 There are enormous ____ like Everest in Nepal.
a mountains b deserts
c beaches

4 There's an ice sheet in ____ .
a Greenland b Brazil
c Australia

5 You use a ____ to wash clothes.
a dishwasher
b washing machine
c refrigerator

6 You use a ____ to surf the internet.
a console b browser
c webcam

7 You use a ____ to store clothes.
a carpet b curtain
c closet

8 After you wash and dry shirts, you need to ____ them.
a mop b clean c iron

9 A guitar is a kind of ____ .
a device b instrument
c appliance

10 You need knives and forks to ____ the table.
a set b clean c wash

3 Complete the circles with the words in the box.

ant bear bee crocodile
human ~~dolphin~~ lion owl
parrot penguin snake turtle

birds	insects	reptiles	mammals
			dolphin

ALL ABOUT ME

1 **What's your favorite animal?**

2 **What animal(s) are you scared of?**

3 **What's your favorite place?**

4 **What places do you want to visit?**

1 Complete the sentences with the simple past or past progressive form of the verb in parentheses.

1 I ______ (watch) a TV show about lions when you ______ (call).
2 Sue ______ (eat) dinner when she ______ (see) a mouse under the table.
3 While Luke ______ (hike) in Australia, he ______ (take) a lot of pictures.
4 Tony ______ (swim) near the beach when he ______ (hear) a loud noise.
5 When we ______ (be) on vacation in Mexico last year, we ______ (find) a deserted island.
6 I ______ (sit) in a café when a famous actor ______ (come) in.

2 Choose the correct options from the box below to complete the conversation.

Martin: What (1) ______ doing while (2) ______ watching the video in class today? (3) ______ drawing pictures?
Klara: No, I (4) ______ ! I (5) ______ drawing a mind map.
Martin: A mind map? What's that?
Klara: It's a way to organize my notes. I (6) ______ mind maps when I listen to lectures or presentations. When I review (7) ______ map later, I can remember the ideas better too.
Martin: That sounds good. I (8) ______ so lazy about taking notes. So how (9) ______ make a mind map?
Klara: Well, first I (10) ______ the main idea in a square or circle like this. Then I (11) ______ lines to connect it with other circles and put key words on each line.
Martin: Hm, OK. Why (12) ______ capital letters?
Klara: Capital letters are for important ideas. You can use symbols and colors too.
Martin: I could try that! So … what (13) ______ after (14) ______ lecture tomorrow?
Klara: Why do you want to know?
Martin: Well, I thought we could compare notes!

	a	b		a	b
1	were you	you were	8	always am	am always
2	were we	we were	9	you do	do you
3	Were you	You were	10	write	am writing
4	didn't	wasn't	11	draw	am drawing
5	were	was	12	you use	do you use
6	usually draw	draw usually	13	do you do	are you doing
7	a	the	14	the	–

3 Complete the sentences with the correct form of the verbs in the box.

do (x2) get home go go fishing go shopping

1 What ______ on Friday afternoons?
2 Where ______ on vacation this summer?
3 We're ______ on Sunday. I want to buy a dress.
4 We usually ______ at around 6:00 p.m.
5 What ______ right now?
6 I'm ______ tomorrow morning.

4 WHAT'S COOKING?

UNIT 4

VOCABULARY 1 >>> Kitchen equipment and cooking verbs

1 a Find the food and drinks in the word snake. Then complete the lists with the words.

mineralwaterlemononioneggsbreadteachickenjuicepotatobananacarrotapplemilktomatocoffee

vegetables ....
drinks *mineral water*
fruits ....
other ....

b Add two fruits, two vegetables, and two drinks to the lists.

2 Complete the words.

1 
k ____

2 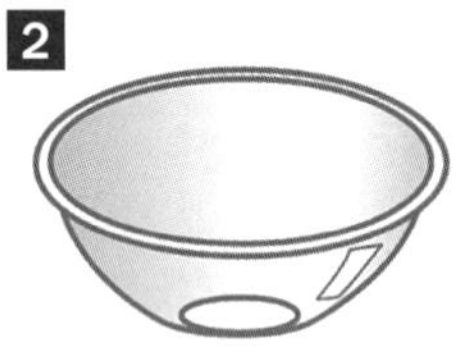
b ____

3 
f ____
p ____

4 
s ____

5 
c ____
b ____

3 Match the sentence parts.

1 You use a frying pan to
2 You use a saucepan to
3 You use a cutting board to
4 You use a bowl to
5 You use a knife to

a cook foods like soup, rice, or pasta.
b cut vegetables into pieces.
c beat or stir things in before cooking.
d cut food on.
e cook foods like eggs, meat, and fish in oil.

4 a Complete the recipe with the verbs in the box.

beat chop fry heat pour stir

1 .... the eggs in a large bowl, then cover them.
2 Carefully .... the vegetables with a sharp knife.
3 .... some oil in a frying pan.
4 .... the potatoes until they are golden brown.
5 Add the onions and .... the mixture.
6 Then .... in the eggs from the bowl.

b What's your favorite meal to make at home? What ingredients do you need to make it?

....

....

5 Write the missing letters to make words. Then check your answers by finding them in the word search.

MENU

Main courses:
(1) ____ with fries
Tomato and (2) ____ pizza
Homemade (3) ____
Selection of (4) ____

Extras:
bread and (5) ____ , (6) ____

Desserts:
(7) ____ ____ , (8) ____ cake
Fruit (9) ____ with apples, (10) ____
and (11) ____

a	p	e	r	w	b	i	y	b	z
s	a	n	d	w	i	c	h	e	s
t	s	g	r	a	p	e	s	u	y
e	t	k	j	x	e	c	w	v	r
a	a	t	k	h	y	r	n	b	m
k	c	y	u	c	h	e	e	s	e
f	r	i	e	s	s	a	l	a	d
b	u	t	t	e	r	m	i	o	p
x	z	q	o	r	a	n	g	e	s
m	c	h	o	c	o	l	a	t	e

READING

Use headings to find specific information

1 Read the introduction to Adam's blog below. Is he a good cook? ______

2 Read Adam's text quickly. What's he making?

a a sandwich b an omelette c a large meal

3 Complete the tips with the correct imperatives from the box.

REMEMBER HOW TO …

use headings to find specific information

decide find read (x2)

1 ______ what information you need.
2 ______ the headings (and first sentence if necessary).
3 ______ the correct heading and ______ the information under this heading.

4 Put the headings in the correct place in the recipe.

Directions Time Things you need Notes Ingredients

5 Choose the correct option to complete the sentences.

1 You can make Adam's Kitchen Creation in ______ time.
  a a lot of
  b not much
  c few
2 You don't need a ______ to make this recipe.
  a knife
  b frying pan
  c bowl
3 Cook the eggs for ______ minutes.
  a ten
  b five
  c three
4 Adam says that his recipe is not ______ to make.
  a easy
  b difficult
  c cheap
5 To make the meal larger, you can add ______ .
  a a salad
  b ketchup
  c butter
6 Adam says that sandwiches in ______ can have a lot of layers.
  a Greece
  b the USA
  c Lebanon

MOVE BEYOND

Find a recipe online. Write headings, then add notes next to each heading.

______
______
______
______

Hi, I'm Adam. I'm a student at Lincoln College. I'm living away from home for the first time, and it's not easy! I love eating, but I'm not sure about cooking. This is one of my easy Kitchen Creations! I hope you like it.

Adam's Kitchen Creations #1

(1) ______: 10 minutes
Level of difficulty: simple
Serves: me!

(2) ______
2 eggs
a little cheese
50ml oil
some bread

(3) ______
knife
cutting board
frying pan

(4) ______
1 First, heat the oil in a small frying pan.
2 Carefully break the eggs into the frying pan, and stir.
3 After that, stir the eggs in the frying pan for three minutes. Then turn off the heat.
4 Cut pieces of cheese, and then cut some bread.
5 Put the cheese on the bread – you don't need butter.
6 Add the eggs from the frying pan.
7 If you're more creative, add some more ingredients. For example, tomatoes or even meat.
8 Enjoy!

(5) ______
This is my favorite recipe because there are only a few ingredients, and it's super quick and cheap!

I like adding some ketchup, or salt and pepper, to my Kitchen Creation.

You can make your meal healthier (and bigger!) with a salad! Mix lettuce, tomatoes, carrots, and onions with oil and lemon juice. Eat your salad with your sandwich.

Fact! People all over the world eat sandwiches. In Greece and Lebanon, they sometimes use "pitas" (thin bread) for their sandwiches. In the USA, "club sandwiches" have a lot of layers.

GRAMMAR 1 Expressions of quantity

Talk about quantity

1 Complete the grammar table with the correct forms.

	Countable (e.g., *eggs*)	**Uncountable** (e.g., *cheese*)
+	(1) s……, no, (2) a f……, (3) a l…… of	some, no, (6) a l……, a lot of
-	any, (4) m……, a lot of	(7) a……, (8) m……, a lot of
?	(5) a……, many, a few, a lot of	any, (9) m……, (10) a l……, a lot of

2 Look at the table in Exercise 1 and complete the rules with the words in the box.

countable uncountable countable and uncountable (x2)

1 Use *not many* and (*a*) *few* with plural …… nouns.
2 Use *not much* and (*a*) *little* with …… nouns.
3 Use *a lot of* and *some* with …… nouns.
4 Use *no* with …… nouns.

3 a Complete the table with the nouns in the box.

~~banana~~ cheese egg juice lemon milk oil pasta potato rice sandwich soda tea vegetable

Countable	Uncountable
banana	

b Add two words to each list.

4 Put the expressions of quantity in the correct circles.

a few a little a lot of many much ~~no~~ not many not much some

zero	**a small quantity**	**not a small or large quantity**	**a large quantity**
no			

5 Choose the correct option to complete the sentences.

1 *There's* / *There are* a little cheese.
2 *There's* / *There isn't* no bread.
3 *Are* / *Is* there a lot of vegetables?
4 I *have* / *don't have* much chocolate.
5 *Are* / *Is* there any coffee?
6 *There's* / *There isn't* any food in the refrigerator.

6 › Choose one correct option to describe the nouns.

1 *some* / *a few* bread
2 *some* / *a little* vegetables
3 *a few* / *a lot of* fruit
4 *not many* / *some* rice
5 *not many* / *not much* eggs
6 *some* / *many* orange juice

7 › Complete the conversation with the expressions of quantity.

an a few (x2) a little (x2) not much

Sam: Hey Amy!
Amy: Hi Sam!
Sam: What are you doing?
Amy: I'm making (1) .... omelette.
Sam: Yum! I'm hungry. How do you make an omelette Amy?
Amy: Well, you need (2) .... eggs and some oil.
Sam: OK.
Amy: You heat some oil – (3) .... , though – then mix the eggs and stir them in the frying pan.
Sam: Sounds complicated!
Amy: It's easy! After that you add (4) .... salt and pepper.
Sam: That's it?
Amy: You can also add (5) .... vegetables ... or (6) .... cheese.
Sam: Delicious!

8 ›› Complete the sentences with *not much* or *not many* and the verb in parentheses.

1 We .... (eat) vegetables.
2 There .... (be) good restaurants near here.
3 I .... (have) friends at this school.
4 We .... (have) cheese. Can you buy some?
5 We .... (have) homework tonight.
6 I .... (have) time to cook at night.

9 ›› Complete the second sentence so that it has the same meaning as the first.

1 The mall has two cafés.
There .... two cafés at the mall.
2 We don't have many eggs.
There are a .... eggs.
3 There isn't much juice.
There's a .... juice.
4 There isn't any bread.
There's .... bread.
5 There are no eggs on the table.
There aren't .... eggs on the table.
6 There aren't many good recipes in this book.
This book only has a .... good recipes.

10 ››› Write questions and answers.

1 Q: (any / bread) *Is there any bread?*
A: (a little) *There's a little bread.*
2 Q: (any / cheese) ....
A: (not much) ....
3 Q: (any / apples) ....
A: (a few) ....
4 Q: (any / eggs) ....
A: (a few) ....
5 Q: (a little / tea) ....
A: (some) ....
6 Q: (any / grapes) ....
A: (not many) ....

Recognize facts and opinions

1 Read about Martin's home. What materials is he using to make his bedroom wall and kichen furniture?

a boxes and jars
b bottles and cans
c packages and milk cartons

Martin Ramsey is very interested in the environment and recycling. He thinks people don't recycle enough, so he's building his new home from recycled materials. His bedroom and bathroom walls are made from plastic bottles. His kitchen furniture is made from empty cans. The house is an excellent example of really bringing recycling home! Some of his neighbors think it's unhealthy to make a house out of trash, but in my opinion, recycled homes are a great idea!

2 Circle the facts and underline the opinions in Exercise 1. How many are there of each?

Number of facts: ____
Number of opinions: ____

3 81 Listen and choose the percentages and numbers you hear.

30 22 75 17
1,000 2 5,000

4 81 Complete the sentences with information from the listening. Then listen again and check your answers.

1 The show begins at ________ o'clock.
2 ________ percent of trash can be recycled.
3 ________ percent of trash is actually recycled.
4 The local school gave Martin ________ plastic bottles.
5 He needs over ________ cans to make the kitchen furniture.

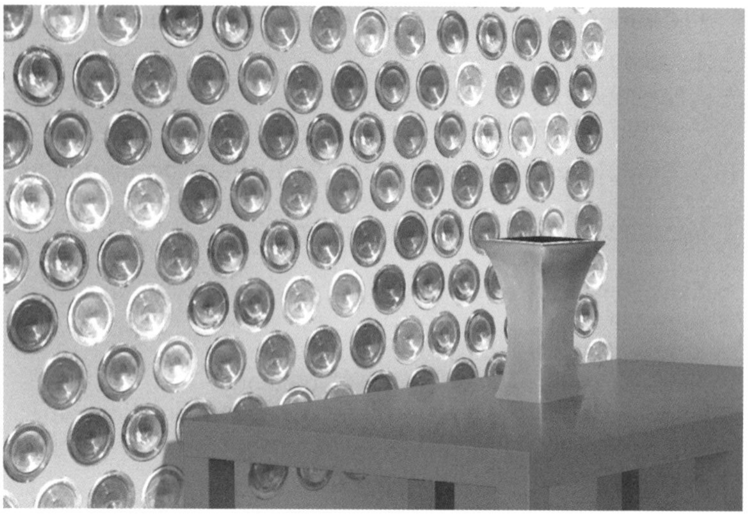

5 a Read the excerpts from the listening text. Say which are facts (*F*) and which are opinions (*O*).

1 Today's show is called *Waste Not, Want Not*. ____
2 Later, we will see if people think it's a good idea. ____
3 Seventy-five percent of trash can be recycled. ____
4 People make a lot of excuses not to recycle. ____
5 To make the kitchen table and chairs, I need over 5,000 cans. ____

b 81 Listen again find one more fact and one more opinion.

____
____

6 Look at the different ideas about recycling. Check (✓) the ones you think are good ideas. Think of two more ideas.

1 Throw all waste into one big trash can.
2 Tell people recycling is very complicated and a lot of work.
3 Think about ways to use recycled material, for example, to build houses.
4 Give friends and neighbors tips on how to recycle.

____
____

Containers and amounts

1 Rearrange the words to complete Rebecca and Ethan's shopping lists.

Rebecca

2 x cans of u p s o (1) ....

1 x carton of e c j u i r a n o e g (2) ....

1 x box of t e s c h c o l o a (3) ....

(for Ali)

2 x pieces of m e t a (steak?) (4) ....

1 x carton of g s g e (5) ....

1 x bottle of olive l i o (6) ....

Salt

Ethan

9:30

YOUR SHOPPING LIST

- Loaf of **b e a d r** (a) ....
- 6 bottles of **w e r a t** (b) ....
- Package of **a s t p a** (c) ....
- A few vegetables – tomatoes, carrots
- Jar of strawberry **m j a** (d) ....
- Carton of **c i e r e m c a** (e) ....
- Piece of **h e c e s e** (f) ....

2 Look at Exercise 1. Who is a vegetarian? Who is allergic to dairy?

Vegetarian .... Allergic to dairy ....

3 a Label the pictures with the containers and the type of food/drink.

1 a .... of ....

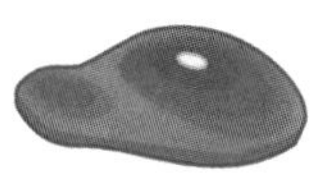

2 a .... of ....

3 a .... of ....

4 a .... of ....

5 a .... of ....

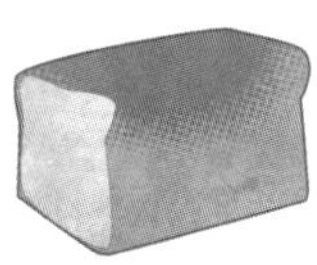

6 a .... of ....

7 a .... of ....

8 a .... of ....

b Which of the things in Exercise 3a do you have in your refrigerator at home?

4 Find and correct six mistakes in the conversation. Write the correct sentences below.

Rebecca: Hey, Ethan! Ready to go shopping?
Ethan: Yeah, just a second. Are there any eggs in the refrigerator?
Rebecca: Yes, there's a can of eggs in the refrigerator. What else do we need?
Ethan: Check and see if there's any butter.
Rebecca: Let's see. Yes, there are two bottles of butter next to this carton of cake.
Ethan: Perfect. What about soup?
Rebecca: Uh, no, there's no soup.
Ethan: OK, let's get some. And ... is there any bread?
Rebecca: Yes, there's a jar of bread in the cabinet. There's also a piece of oil and a loaf of rice.

1 ....
2 ....
3 ....
4 ....
5 ....
6 ....

WORDS & BEYOND

Find the odd word out in each group. Write down why it's different.

1 cookies cakes chicken pancakes
....

2 milkshake ice cream cream coffee
....

3 flour butter soda eggs
....

4 salt pepper milk spices
....

5 lemons jam grapes oranges
....

6 throw away recycle take out eat
....

GRAMMAR 2 Indefinite pronouns

»»» Use indefinite pronouns

1 › Complete the grammar table with the correct forms.

People	Things	Places	Examples
(1) *somebody* or someone	something	(2)	Somebody/Someone is waiting for you outside. There's something on the table for you. We need to choose somewhere to go on vacation.
anybody or (3)	anything	(4)	I can't see anybody/anyone in the classroom. There isn't anything on the table. Is there anywhere I can buy a bottle of water?
(5) .... or (6)	(7)	everywhere	Everybody/Everyone loved the party. I have everything I need for the cake. Everywhere I go people help me.
(8) .... or (9)	nothing	(10)	Nobody/No one came to the party. There's nothing in the refrigerator. I have nowhere to go after class.

2 › Choose the correct option to complete the rules.

1 Indefinite pronouns (*anything*, *nobody*) ***refer*** / ***don't refer*** to a specific person, thing, or place.
2 Use *some-* and *no-* in **negative** / ***affirmative*** sentences.
3 Use *any-* in questions and ***negative*** / ***affirmative*** sentences.
4 Use *every-* with ***singular*** / ***plural*** verbs.

3 »› Choose the correct option to complete the sentences.

1 ***No one*** / ***Anyone*** in my family recycles.
2 I don't have ***something*** / ***anything*** in my school bag that I can recycle.
3 Is there ***everywhere*** / ***anywhere*** that I can recycle this bottle?
4 ***Somebody*** / ***Everybody*** left their bag in the classroom.
5 There's ***everything*** / ***nothing*** in the recycling bin.
6 Has ***anybody*** / ***something*** seen my pen?

4 »»› Complete the blog with indefinite pronouns.

ROSEWOOD
RECYCLES!

Thanks to the hard work of students in the eighth grade at Rosewood School, next year (1) .... in the school is going to start recycling.
Right now only 40% of classrooms have recycling bins. Some students recycle a lot, and some don't recycle (2) .... But next year bins are going to be (3) .... – in classrooms, hallways, and on the school grounds.

The eighth graders think (4) .... is more important than the environment. You can recycle at home and at school – it's easy and simple. Andrew, the president of the Recycling Club says, (5) "........ should recycle – it's important and very easy! So do (6) .... about it today. Why not ask (7) .... from the eighth grade to tell you about it? Put recycling boxes in your classroom for a start. Last year, (8) .... in our class understood how recycling works, but now we're changing the whole school!"

Congratulations to (9) .... from the Recycling Club for bringing this great idea to Rosewood!

5 »»› a Complete the poem with the correct indefinite pronouns.

Hands up (1) .... ,
There's (2) .... we
can do!
Recycling is important
For me and for you!

Does (3) .... have ideas
So we can make the plan?
Let's look (4) .... for
things to recycle
All around the town.

Hands up (5) .... ,
Do (6) .... right away!
Recycling is important
For tomorrow and today.

b Do you agree with the poem's message?

Express preferences when you order food

1 a Match the questions to the answers.

1 Can you repeat your address, please? b
2 How can I help you? ____
3 Would you like some chicken on your salad? ____
4 OK, what's your name and address? ____
5 What's the special today? ____

a No thanks, I'm a vegetarian.
b 13 Aragon Road.
c I'd like to place a take-out order, please.
d We have the Tomato Salad and our Chef's Salad.
e It's Maria. I live at 13 Aragon Road.

b Circle the polite words.

2 ▶82 Put the conversation in Exercise 1 in order. Then listen and check your answers.

1 2c
2 ____
3 ____
4 ____
5 ____

3 ▶82 Listen to the phone conversation again and complete the sentences.

1 Sammy works at ____ .
2 Maria is calling from ____ .
3 Maria orders a ____ .
4 The order includes ____ chips or bread.
5 Maria is ____ to flour.
6 Sammy asks Maria to ____ her address.

4 Circle the polite form of each request. Then practice repeating the polite phrases.

1 a What?
b Can you repeat that, please?
2 a I want to place an order.
b I'd like to place an order.
3 a What do you want?
b What would you like?
4 a Do you have any steak?
b Where's the steak?
5 a Can I have the vegetable soup?
b Give me the vegetable soup.
6 a I want apple juice instead.
b I'd prefer apple juice.

5 ▶83 Complete the conversation below with the phrases in the box. Then listen and check.

Can I have	Can I help	Could you say
Do you have	I'd like	I'd rather	please
sorry	thank you	Would you like

Sarah: Let's stop here and get something to eat before we get to Marco's house.
Nick: Good idea!
Man: Hello there. (1) ____ you?
Nick: Let me see. (2) ____ an egg salad sandwich with lettuce and tomato.
Sarah: (3) ____ the same but with no lettuce, please?
Man: Of course. (4) ____ some cold drinks?
Nick: (5) ____ any soda?
Man: No, sorry. I have cartons of juice or bottles of water.
Sarah: (6) ____ have iced tea.
Nick: One bottle of water and one glass of iced tea, (7) ____ .
Man: OK, that's $7.70.
Sarah: Thank you. Oh, and can you tell us where Marigold Avenue is?
Man: (8) ____ ? Mari*grove* Avenue? (9) ____ that again, please?
Sarah: Marigold Avenue – M-A-R-I-G-O-L-D.
Man: Oh, yes. It's just around the corner.
Nick and Sarah: (10) ____ !

6 ▶84 PRONOUNCE Listen and complete the phrases. Mark the stressed syllables. Then practice repeating the phrases.

1 a bottle of milk
2 a ____ of ____
3 a ____ of ____
4 a ____ of ____
5 a ____ of ____

Order ideas

1 Number the steps in the correct order.

...... Finally, put all the paper and cardboard into the green recycling bin.
...... Next, fold the cardboard and flatten the egg boxes.
...... First, wash the glass bottles.
...... Then, put the clean bottles into the blue recycling bin.

2 Match the two parts of the sentences to make tips.

1 Use *first*
2 Use *next*, *then*, or *after that*
3 Use *finally*

a for steps 2, 3, or 4.
b for the last step.
c for step 1.

3 Underline five sequencers in the instructions.

My uncle is visiting. He's teaching me to make something special. It's a typical dish called Cuban-style rice. I love trying new food.

"Pay attention, Joseph. Here's everything you need to make Cuban-style rice: some oil, one egg, two cups of rice, six tomatoes, and two onions. Add spices and plantains to make it even better!

First, you need to cook the rice with water in a saucepan. It takes about 15 minutes. Next, prepare some tomato sauce. Stir in the fried onions and spices. Then, heat a little oil in the frying pan and fry the egg. When the rice is ready, put it on a plate and make a hole in the middle. After that, pour some tomato sauce into the hole. Finally, put the fried egg on top. And here's a tip – add pieces of plantain to make it even more special!"

4 Rearrange the words to make instructions.

1 boil / first / water / the .

....

2 tea bag / put / cup / next / in / a / a .

....

3 pour / that / the / boiling water / after / tea bag / onto / the .

....

4 take out / tea bag / the / then .

....

5 next / milk / some / add .

....

6 sugar / finally / stir in / some .

....

5 **Your friends are organizing a birthday party and they need your help. Order your ideas in a plan. Use the *Ideas box* and the *Writing plan* to help you prepare.**

IDEAS BOX

cake clean your house food and drinks go shopping ice cream pizza presents sandwiches talk to your friends

WRITING PLAN

Make notes for your party plan.

1 Who is the birthday party for?

____

2 What do you do the day before the party? Think of three things.

____

____

____

3 What food do you make for the party?

____

____

____

4 Use sequencers to order your ideas.

____

WRITE AND CHECK

6 **Write your instructions. Check (✓) the stages in the *Writing plan*.**

Plan for ________ 's birthday party.

Consider other people's needs and preferences

1 **Read the email. What is Tom organizing?**

____

2 **Read the text messages that each person sent Tom. Whose needs and preferences are most important? Put them in order, from 1 (most important) to 5 (least important).**

a ☐ Do I have to share with Diego? You know we're not very good friends! – **Esteban**

b ☐ Sorry Tom, I hurt my foot yesterday. Can I be close to the bathroom? – **Daniel**

c ☐ Sounds good to me Tom! I'm happy to share with anybody! Can't wait! – **Miguel**

d ☐ Everybody knows I'm a light sleeper. I really can't share with anyone. Can you change my room? – **Gilbert**

e ☐ Please, please, please, can I share with you and Miguel?! ☺ – **Diego**

Hey guys!

I figured out the rooms in the hostel for next week! This is who's sharing and who's not!

Room 1 (double room, with its own bathroom): Esteban and Diego.

Room 2 (triple room, shared bathroom): Daniel, Gilbert, and Miguel.

Room 3 (single room, shared bathroom): Me!

I hope everyone's happy with this!

Tom

3 **What is wrong with Tom's plan? In your notebook, reorganize the rooms considering each person's needs and preferences.**

4 **What else can Tom ask the hostel to do to help Daniel and Gilbert?**

____

____

____

RESPECT OTHERS

1 Complete the table with the words in the box.

clear the table cook dinner ~~go shopping~~ go swimming listen to music load the dishwasher meet friends play the piano read a book ride a bike set the table sort the recycling take out the trash walk the dog

Free-time activities	Household chores
go shopping	

2 Complete the puzzle. Use the notes to help you.

1		E	E				
2			Y				
3		O					
4				K			
5	S						
6				I			
7						D	
8	B						
9		R					
10			N		T		

1 insect that makes honey
2 thing that opens doors
3 bread in a long or round shape
4 drink that makes cheese and butter
5 reptile that doesn't have any legs
6 machine for listening to music and news
7 small piece of land, in the middle of the ocean
8 yellow fruit that grows on trees
9 boy who has the same parents as you
10 part of computer that contains the screen

3 Complete the table with the words in the box.

ant butter calculator desert flour furniture grass hall hill milk printer sneakers trash

Countable	Uncountable

ALL ABOUT ME

1 What food do you cook at home?

2 What things do you recycle (a) at home and (b) at school? Make a list.

3 What are your favorite free-time activities?

1 Choose the correct options to complete the text.

Last Sunday I had (1) ***a*** / ***the*** picnic lunch with my friends in the park. I took (2) ***some*** / ***much*** sandwiches and (3) ***a little*** / ***a few*** apples. I brought (4) ***a*** / ***the*** bottle of juice to drink. My friends brought (5) ***much*** / ***a lot of*** sweet things: (6) **–** / ***the*** cookies, (7) ***a*** / ***the*** cake and (8) ***two*** / ***some*** chocolate. There was so (9) ***much*** / ***many*** food!

2 Complete the text with the correct form of the verbs in the box.

be call not be pass see sit think walk

While I (1) .... home from school yesterday, I (2) .... an accident between two bicyclists. A lot of people (3) .... by, so someone immediately (4) .... the police on a cell phone. The accident (5) .... serious, but I saw that one of the bicyclists (6) .... on the grass waiting for help because she had a small cut on her head. I (7) .... she was fine, though. She (8) .... smiling and talking.

3 Complete the text with the correct pronouns.

"This week (1) .... are starting the new recycling campaign at our school and (2) .... is taking part!

As (3) .... can see, there are now recycling bins (4) .... at school: in the classrooms, on the school grounds, and in the cafeteria. When you see (5) .... with trash, please tell them to use the bins!

Does (6) .... have any questions? OK. I don't have (7) .... else to add. Good luck and happy recycling!"

4 Write questions for the answers.

1 Q: *What are you reading?*
A: I'm reading a newspaper.

2 Q: ....
A: The class is 40 minutes long.

3 Q: ....
A: No, there aren't any eggs in the refrigerator.

4 Q: ....
A: Yes, I eat a lot of fruit.

5 Q: ....
A: I play soccer every Sunday.

6 Q: ....
A: I went to Chile last summer.

5 Rearrange the words to make sentences.

1 hardly ever / I / to the movies / go .
I hardly ever go to the movies.

2 is / in her room / doing / her homework / Maggie .
....

3 your bed / do / How often / you / make ?
....

4 go / Did / you / the coffee shop / yesterday / to ?
....

5 driving / to the mall / They / when / were / a car / into them / crashed .
....

6 didn't go / last week / to / They / the movies .
....

UNIT 5

WHO AM I?

VOCABULARY 1 >>>> Personality adjectives

1 Match the adjectives to their opposites.

1 funny a brave
2 confident b rude
3 polite c shy
4 scared d serious

2 a Complete the descriptions with the adjectives in the box.

brave creative generous
kind sensitive smart

1 Sara always volunteers to help other people. She's very ________ .
2 Dan always thinks of unusual new ideas. He's ________ .
3 Tanya isn't afraid of anything. She's ________ .
4 My big brother usually pays for my lunch. He's so ________ .
5 Lucy cries at sad movies. She's ________ .
6 Simon and Andy are very good at all the school subjects. They're very ________ .

b Describe your ideal friend. What is he or she like? Use three adjectives.

________ ________ ________

3 Choose the correct option to complete the sentences.

1 I'm too shy. I want to be more ***confident*** / ***competitive***.
2 I'm afraid of everything. I want to be ***ambitious*** / ***brave***.
3 I don't have any new ideas. I want to be more ***creative*** / ***smart***.
4 I don't have a goal for the future. I want to be ***ambitious*** / ***confident***.
5 I'm not good at any subjects. I want to be ***brave*** / ***smart***.
6 I never win anything. I want to be ***creative*** / ***competitive***.

4 a Look at the quiz. For options a and b write the best word from the box below.

calm cheerful competitive friendly funny generous
kind polite ~~rude~~ sensitive serious shy

b Take the quiz. What are your results? Do you agree?

____

____

WHAT ARE YOU LIKE?

Find out about your personality with our personality quiz.

Quizzes About Forums

1 Your friend asks you for money. What do you say?
a "Forget it!" *rude* b "Of course! How much do you need?" ________
2 Your best friend doesn't want to talk to you. What do you do?
a Start to cry. ________ b Ask them quietly about the problem. ________
3 You have won second place in a contest. How do you feel?
a You have to do better next time. ________ b Pleased and happy – it's no problem! ________
4 Your friend calls you very early in the morning and wakes you up. What do you say?
a "What's wrong? Are you OK?" ________
b "It's a little early. Could you please call back later? Thanks so much." ________
5 A new student joins your class. What do you do?
a Introduce yourself and say hello. ________ b Smile, but wait for them to say hello. ________
6 Your teacher asks you to speak to the class about your favorite subject. What do you choose?
a Tell some jokes. ________ b Relax and talk about your plans for the future. ________

Identify the goal of a text

1 a Look at the title of the magazine article and the five different shapes (a–e). Write the names of the shapes under them.

b Check (✓) the shapes that you like best.

square ☐ rectangle ☐ triangle ☐
circle ☐ squiggle ☐

2 Read the title, look at the diagrams, and read the first line of each paragraph. Then answer the questions.

1 What kind of text is it?
a an advertisement
b a personal story
c an article

2 What are the pictures in the text for?
a they add extra information
b they show what important words in the text mean
c they aren't there for any special reason

3 What is the main topic of the text?
a how to change your personality
b how to understand your personality
c how to improve your personality

4 What is the goal of the text?
a to give information
b to advertise
c to give an opinion

3 At work, what is each person in the article probably very good at doing? For 1–5, choose the best answer.

1 Being friendly to customers. circle
2 Completing long, difficult tasks. ....
3 Thinking of new ideas. ....
4 Getting things done in good time. ....
5 Making the business very successful. ....

4 Match the definitions to the underlined words and phrases in the text.

1 cheerful ....
2 nervous ....
3 not late ....
4 peace and happiness ....
5 small but important things ....
6 not shy ....

5 Match the best personality adjective to each shape.

ambitious calm creative friendly shy

1 ....
2  ....
3  ....
4  ....
5  ....

WHAT SHAPE IS YOUR PERSONALITY?

Are you a square, a rectangle, a triangle, a circle, or a squiggle? This simple symbol test can help you understand your own personality and your work style!

a square

The **Square** …
is serious and organized. This type of person works hard to finish a task even if it's boring. The **square** is good at concentrating and doesn't often feel worried.

The **Rectangle** …
is also organized, but will try to create a system with rules to make sure everything is finished. The **rectangle** is usually on time, but this person isn't always good at making friends.

b ....

c ....

The **Triangle** …
is ambitious and competitive. This person will aim to reach a goal but might not notice all the details. The final goal is very important to this person. The **triangle** always loves to get attention.

The **Circle** …
is social and good at communicating. This person likes harmony in the workplace and gets everyone working together. Organization and planning are not the most important things for this person. The **circle** is always in a good mood.

d ....

The **Squiggle** …
likes to invent new things and can think of interesting solutions to problems. This person gets bored with doing the same thing all the time. The **squiggle** gets excited easily.

e ....

Understanding your personality is an important part of living a happy life. It can help you understand your friends and family and help you choose a job you like.

MOVE BEYOND

Find and complete a free personality test online. What was your result?

Your result: ....

Do you agree? Why or why not? ....

GRAMMAR 1 Adjectives with prepositions + *-ing* form

Express your feelings about doing things

1 Complete the grammar tables with the correct forms.

Pronoun	Verb	Adjective	Preposition	*-ing* form of verb/noun
I	am ('m)	good/bad	(1) ______	 painting.
She	(2) ______	not so good	at	 (3) ______ .
He	(4) ______	excited	about	 (5) going ______ on Saturday.
We	(6) ______	bored	with	 (7) ______ .
They	are/'re	excited	(8) ______	 cooking Sunday dinner.

Questions				
(9) ______	they	interested	(10) ______	 (11) ______ comic books?
Are	you	tired	(12) ______	 taking pictures?
Why are	they	worried	(13) ______	 the homework?
What (14) ______	you	scared	of	doing?

2 Choose the correct option to complete the rules.

1 After an adjective + a preposition, use the *-ing* / *infinitive* form of the verb.
2 After an adjective + preposition, use ***an adjective*** / ***a noun***.
3 For one-syllable verbs that end in a single vowel + consonant, ***double*** / ***remove*** the consonant before you add *-ing*
4 If a verb ends in *-e*, ***remove*** / ***don't remove*** the *e* before you add *-ing*.
5 ***Always*** / ***Never*** double the consonant for verbs ending in *w* or *x*.

3 Write the *-ing* form of the verbs.

1 draw *drawing*
2 tell ______
3 read ______
4 swim ______
5 write ______
6 take ______
7 create ______
8 use ______
9 run ______
10 cook ______

4 Choose the correct options to complete the conversation.

Teacher: Hi, Mrs. Wilson. Thanks for coming in with Alison to talk about her schoolwork.
Mrs. Wilson: Hello, Mrs. Green. I'm worried (1) ***about*** / ***with*** Alison's grades. They aren't so good this semester, are they?
Teacher: Well, let's see. Alison is very interested (2) ***in*** / ***of*** music and art. Those are her favorite subjects. But she isn't very interested (3) ***at*** / ***in*** doing her math homework! I'm tired (4) ***about*** / ***of*** reminding her!
Mrs. Wilson: Oh dear, and what about English? Is she good (5) ***at*** / ***on*** reading and writing?
Teacher: Well, she's not bad (6) ***about*** / ***at*** reading and writing, but she's very good (7) ***at*** / ***with*** talking!
Alison: I'm really good (8) ***at*** / ***with*** history and geography, though! And I'm really excited (9) ***about*** / ***in*** that new history project we're doing!
Teacher: Yes, that's true. Your project is looking really good.
Mrs. Wilson: You sometimes get bored (10) ***on*** / ***with*** studying for tests. Isn't that true, Alison?
Alison: Yes, I guess so ...

5 Complete the sentences about Alison. Use the correct preposition and a phrase from the box.

Alison's grades	her history project
math	reading and writing
studying for tests	talking

1 Mrs. Wilson is worried ______ .
2 Alison is very good ______ .
3 She isn't interested ______ .
4 She's not bad ______ .
5 She's excited ______ .
6 She's bored ______ .

6 › Complete the email with the adjectives in the box.

bored excited good interested scared tired worried (x2)

Dear Julie,
I'm starting a new sport – judo! I'm really (1) ________ at doing athletics, but I was (2) ________ with running and (3) ________ of long jump and I want to try something new. I'm a little bit (4) ________ about the first class. Will it be very difficult? I'm not (5) ________ about falling down, but I'm a little bit (6) ________ of hurting someone else! Anyway I'm really (7) ________ about joining the club. I think it'll be a lot of fun. Are you (8) ________ in going with me?
See you soon,
Jessica

7 ›› Complete the ads with the words in the box.

bored good interested scared tired worried

International cooking
(1) ________ of cooking the same thing all the time? Develop your cooking skills by learning to prepare international dishes from Mexico, India, and Thailand.

Web design group
(4) ________ in creating your own website? Join our web design group and see how easy it is!

SINGING CLUB
(2) ________ at singing? Join our singing club once a week and make friends through music!

Apps and games club
(5) ________ with the same old computer games? Learn how to make your own apps and games.

STUDY GROUP
(3) ________ about passing your exams? Improve your study skills in our school study group. Results guaranteed!

MUSIC GROUP
(6) ________ of playing in front of an audience? Become confident in our music group.

8 ›› Complete the sentences with a preposition and the correct form of the verb in parentheses. Which club from Exercise 7 should each person join?

1 Martin loves food, but he's not very good *at cooking* (cook). *International cooking*
2 Rebecca studies a lot, but she's still scared ________ (fail) her exams. ________
3 Hanna writes a blog and is really excited ________ (create) her own website. ________
4 Vicky plays guitar, but she's tired ________ (play) music alone. ________
5 Sam is interested ________ (design) some new computer games. ________
6 Lucia loves singing, but she's worried ________ (sing) with other people. ________

9 ››› Complete the second sentence so that it has the same meaning as the first.

1 Alison's a terrible singer.
She's *terrible at singing.*
2 Mike's a good guitar player.
He's ________ the guitar.
3 Susan's learning how to take pictures, because it's interesting.
She's ________ pictures.
4 Ellen thinks that homework is boring.
She's ________ homework.
5 I'm starting at a new school next week – it's exciting!
I'm ________ my new school.
6 Vicky thinks ice hockey is scary.
She's ________ ice hockey.

10 a ››› Use the prompts to write sentences in the simple present.

1 We / not so good / paint .
____
2 You / excited / the party ?
____
3 They / worried / change schools .
____
4 What / Melissa / interested ?
____
5 I / scared / snakes .
____
6 My brother / not bad / swimming .
____

b ››› What are you good at? What are you worried about? What are you scared of?

____

LISTENING

Recognize when speakers need time to think

1 What do you think the proverb below means? Write the meaning in your own words.

Home is where the heart is.

Your definition: ....

....

....

2 a (85) Listen to four students talk about the meaning of this proverb. Where does each person live?

1 .... 3 ....

2 .... 4 ....

b Listen again. Match the students (1–4) to their opinions (a–d).

	Home is ...
1 Aura	a where you're happy.
2 Luiza	b with someone you love.
3 Carlos	c with your family.
4 Yumiko	d where you feel comfortable.

3 (85) Listen again. Complete the information with the names of the countries.

1 Aura was born in ....
2 Luiza was born in ....
3 Carlos was born in ....
4 Yumiko was born in ....

4 a Decide if the sentences are correct (*C*) or incorrect (*I*). Rewrite the incorrect sentences.

1 Aura wants to go back to India. *I*
Aura wants to stay in the USA.
2 Luiza is studying at college. ......
3 Luiza wants to go back to London. ......
4 Carlos doesn't like living in Australia. ......
5 Carlos wants to go to Japan. ......
6 Yumiko doesn't like her home right now. ......

b Listen again and check your answers.

5 Add some hesitation words or sounds to these sentences. Then practice saying them out loud.

1 I want to go to Australia one day.
2 I like traveling and meeting people from different countries.
3 I don't have many brothers and sisters.
4 But I have a lot of really good friends all over the world.

6 What is important to you about your home? Write three ideas and explain why they are important.

....

VOCABULARY 2

Countries, nationalities, and languages

1 Choose the correct option to answer each question.

1 Which country's capital is Kingston?
A Jamaica B France C Canada
2 Which country's capital is Tokyo?
A China B Japan C Korea
3 Which country isn't in Europe?
A Portugal B Brazil C Germany
4 Which country isn't in South America?
A Mexico B Argentina C Brazil
5 Which country speaks Spanish?
A Brazil B Colombia C the Bahamas
6 Which country doesn't speak French?
A France B Egypt C Canada
7 Which country doesn't speak English?
A Singapore B Paraguay C USA
8 Which language do they speak in Egypt?
A English B Egyptian C Arabic

2 Complete the conversation with the correct words.

A: Are you from Argentina?
B: No, I'm from Brazil. I'm ________ .
A: Do you speak Spanish?
B: No, I speak ________ .
A: I'm from Italy, so I speak ________ , but I lived in Mexico for three years, so my ________ is also pretty good.

3 Where are these people (1–10) from? Write the country.

1 We speak Spanish in Mexico.
2 I'm from Tokyo in J______n.
3 I was born in R______a's capital city, Moscow.
4 I'm from a huge country – C______.
5 We love pizza in It______!
6 I was born in F______e's biggest city, Paris.
7 I'm from sunny Sp______!
8 We have a great soccer team in B______l.
9 The pyramids are in my country – Eg______.
10 Winter is cold here in Berlin, Ge______!

4 Now find the nationalities from Exercise 3 in the word search.

M	E	X	I	C	A	N	P	E	J	R
S	E	F	S	M	E	X	B	E	A	L
P	W	U	D	Q	T	T	J	N	P	E
A	S	S	R	L	U	Y	F	M	A	G
N	B	R	A	Z	I	L	I	A	N	Y
I	T	A	L	I	A	N	S	C	E	P
S	X	F	R	E	N	C	H	V	S	T
H	Q	W	I	K	T	F	C	D	E	I
N	L	R	U	S	S	I	A	N	S	A
G	E	R	M	A	N	D	T	S	E	N
H	V	R	C	H	I	N	E	S	E	Q

WORDS & BEYOND

Complete the conversation with the words in the box.

arrows circle doodles patterns
shape square stars triangles

Ana: Caitlin, are you interested in art? Your notebook is covered in (1) ________ !
Caitlin: Haha, it's true! I love drawing (2) ________ and pictures on things.
Ana: What does each (3) ________ mean?
Caitlin: OK, the (4) ________ looks like a television, I guess. And the (5) ________ are a little like mountains … And this big, round (6) ________ is the moon …
Ana: What are the (7) ________ pointing at?
Caitlin: Um, maybe they're pointing up at the (8) ________ ? Honestly, my doodles don't mean anything!

GRAMMAR 2 Hopes, plans, and predictions

Talk about your hopes and plans, and predict events in the future

1 › Complete the grammar tables with the correct forms.

Affirmative				
I	(1) ______	going to	visit	my aunt.
You/We/They	are		take	an exam next year.
He/She/It	(2) ______		have	a party to celebrate.
Negative				
I	am not (3) (______)	going to	visit	my aunt.
You/We/They	are not (aren't)		take	an exam next year.
He/She/It	is not (isn't)		have	a party to celebrate.

Questions					Short answers
Am	I	going to	see	you later?	Yes, I am. / No, (4) ______ .
(5) ______	you/we/they		go	on vacation next week?	Yes, you/we/they are. / No, you/we/they aren't.
Is	he/she		get	good grades?	Yes, (6) ______ . / No, he/she isn't.

2 › Choose the correct option to complete the sentences.

1 What ___ study next year?
a are you going to b will you going to
2 My brother ___ study art.
a will probably b might probably
3 They ___ go to Peru next year.
a will probably b probably are
4 We ___ go to Brazil this year.
a won't probably b probably won't
5 Where ___ going to go tomorrow?
a you're b are you

3 ›› Complete the sentences using the correct form of the words in parentheses. Use contractions, for example, *We're*, where you can.

1 What ______ (going to / you / do) after school?
2 We ______ (not go / probably / will) to the beach because it's too cold.
3 Sue and Leo ______ (cook / going to) dinner for us tonight.
4 We ______ (visit / going to) China next year.
5 ______ (they / come / probably / will) home with us today.
6 They ______ (definitely / not play / will) soccer with us today.

4 ›› Complete the conversation with the words in the box.

~~are you~~ going to hope I'll might probably won't you'll

Isabel: What (1) *are you* going to do this weekend?
Luisa: I'm not sure. I (2) ______ go to the beach, but the weather doesn't look very good, so maybe (3) ______ stay home and study. What about you?
Isabel: I'm (4) ______ practice my song for the school play, but I'm not very good, so I (5) ______ get in.
Luisa: Don't be silly. You're really good at singing! I'm sure (6) ______ get in.
Isabel: Thanks, I (7) ______ I will!

5 a ››› Write sentences using *will*, *definitely*, *probably*, or *may/might*.

1 I want to learn to drive. (100% sure)
I'll definitely learn to drive.
2 We want to visit Italy next year. (50% sure)
______
3 We'll learn Italian next year. (75% sure)
______
4 They won't win the competition. (75% sure)
______
5 Suzanna hopes to study science. (50% sure)
______
6 I want to study harder. (100% sure)
______

b ››› What may/might you do next year? What will you definitely do next year?

______

SPEAKING

Offer help and express spontaneous decisions

1 86 **Number the lines of each conversation in the correct order. Then listen and check your answers.**

Conversation 1:

...... **Matt:** Don't worry. I have this great new book. It explains everything in easy steps. Would you like me to lend it to you?
...... **Matt:** No problem.
1 **Matt:** What's wrong?
...... **Sally:** My math homework is so difficult. I'll never get it done!
...... **Sally:** That would be great! Thanks so much.

Conversation 2:

...... **Katie:** I can practice with you if you like. I'll pretend to be the teacher.
...... **Katie:** I know!
...... **Katie:** What's wrong?
...... **Rob:** I have a music test tomorrow and I'm so nervous!
...... **Rob:** Oh, that's a great idea. That's really nice of you.

2 87 **Listen to the conversations and find different ways to say the phrases (1–4). Then practice repeating the phrases.**

Conversation 1
(1) Would you like me to lend it to you? ......
(2) Thanks so much. ......

Conversation 2
(3) I can practice with you if you like. ......
(4) That's really nice of you. ......

3 a Complete the conversations with the phrases in the box.

I can explain | I can show | I'll show | Would you like me to help | That | That's | would be | you

1 **Dan:** I'm going to a party with my family and friends tomorrow, and I don't know what to wear.
You: ...... you to choose something?
Dan: That ...... great!
2 **Sue:** I have a new cell phone, but I don't understand how it works.
You: Don't worry. ...... you how.
Sue: Thanks. ...... really generous of you!
3 **Jake:** I don't understand the math homework.
You: That's no problem! ...... it to you.
Jake: Oh, thank ....
4 **Gina:** I need to buy a new dictionary, but I don't know which one to get.
You: ...... you my dictionary if you like. It's really good.
Gina: ...... would be great!

b Think of a situation when you offered to help a friend. What did you say?

......

4 88 PRONOUNCE **Complete the table with the nationalities in the box. Then listen and practice repeating the nationalities.**

~~Brazilian~~ English Egyptian German Italian
Japanese Mexican Portuguese Russian Spanish

Syllables			
●••	•●•	••●	●•
	Brazilian		

WRITING

Use *because* and *so*

1 Choose *because* or *so* to complete the rules.

REMEMBER HOW TO ...

use *because* and *so*

- Use ***because*** / ***so*** before a reason (to explain why).
- Use ***because*** / ***so*** before a result (what happens next).

2 Complete each sentence with the correct option.

1 I'm going to learn Spanish because ...
  a I can go to Spain.
  b I like Spanish music.
2 I'm going to join a gym, so ...
  a I can make friends.
  b I need exercise.
3 We're studying graphic design, so ...
  a we can design comic books.
  b we like art.
4 We're getting up early tomorrow because ...
  a we won't be late.
  b we have a test.

3 It's 2033 and Angela is remembering her life in 2015. Read Angela's letter to herself. How old do you think Angela was in 2015?

Dear Me in the Past,

Right now you sometimes feel shy and lonely, but don't be sad! You're really confident inside, and you're very creative. You're very good at art and design. You're excited about new technology and are interested in finding out how to use new computer programs. Concentrate on your skills and you'll feel more confident!

In the future, you're going to have an interesting career in art and design, so you need to study graphic design and learn about computers. You'll also visit a lot of interesting countries, so you need to improve your English! You might want to learn another language, like Spanish or French. Study hard, so you can get good grades and get into college.

I hope you won't feel lonely anymore, because you'll have a lot of friends in the future. You're going to have friends in many different countries because you'll be good at communicating and understanding other people. You're going to be happy and successful, so don't give up!

Love,

Future Angela!

4 Answer the questions using *because* or *so*.

1 Why does Angela sometimes feel sad?
   Because she is sometimes shy and lonely
2 Why does she need to concentrate on the things she's good at?
3 Why does she need to study graphic design?
4 Why does she need to study another language?
5 Why will she have a lot of friends?
6 Why will she be happy?

5 **Imagine that it's 2035, and you're looking back at yourself as you are now. What will you say to the "young you"? Complete the sentences. Then use the *Writing plan* to help you prepare a letter to yourself.**

1 You're good at ______________, so ______________.
2 You're going to ______________ because ______________.
3 I hope you will ______________, so ______________.
4 I hope you won't ______________ because ______________.

WRITING PLAN

Make a plan for your letter.

Dear Me in the Past ...

1 What is your personality like?
______________ ☐
2 What are you good at?
______________ ☐
3 How will those skills be useful in the future?
______________ ☐
4 Which skills do you hope you'll improve on?
______________ ☐
5 What things do you hope you *won't* do? Explain why they are mistakes.
______________ ☐

WRITE AND CHECK

6 **Write your letter. Check (✓) the stages in the plan.**

Recognize what you're good at

1 **Ricardo wants to apply for a summer job as a camp guide in the USA. What skills do you think he needs?** *helping people,* ______________

2 **Read Ricardo's notes. Underline the negative things in his list.**

- bad at spelling and writing in English
- good at speaking English
- no experience working with children (have two little brothers)
- can't drive, have to use my bike
- never been to another country (really want to go!!)
- always on time
- don't like sitting around for long periods ... prefer physical activities like soccer
- not very good at crafts
- can't cook except barbecues! (can make a campfire)

3 **In your notebook rewrite Ricardo's list to turn each negative point into a affirmative sentence.**

4 **Look at the list from Exercise 3. Write a letter (F, S, H, or C) next to each affirmative point.**

F – Helping your family
S – School, learning, and being organized
H – Keeping healthy outdoors
C – Being creative and interested in new things

KNOW YOURSELF

1 Complete the paragraph with the words in the box.

ambitious brave creative ~~France~~ French kind shy Spanish the USA

My name is Sylvie. My mother is from (1) France and my father is from (2) ________ . I speak (3) ________ and English fluently. I like my school, but I'm (4) ________ , so I don't have many friends. My best friend is Louise. Her mother's from Spain, but she doesn't speak (5) ________ . She's very (6) ________ because she always helps me with my problems. She's (7) ________ too because she's not afraid of anything. In the future I'm going to be an artist or a writer because I'm very (8) ________ . I hope I'll be famous one day. I guess I'm pretty (9) ________ too!

2 Read the clues and complete the crossword.

Across

3 You use this to type on your computer. ________

4 She's from Egypt. She speaks ________ .

5 A ________ is an animal and a part of a computer.

6 Milk, cheese, and butter are all types of ________ products.

8 ________ is the opposite of *funny*.

10 You buy water in a ________ .

11 You ________ to music.

Down

1 Snakes are a kind of ________ .

2 You can go walking in the ________ .

7 A ________ is a small computer.

9 You cook dinner in this room: ________ .

3 Find the odd word out in each group. Write down why it's different.

1	fry	chop	play	stir
2	smart	generous	rude	funny
3	Japan	Brazilian	China	France
4	stream	grass	tree	flower
5	compass	calculator	maps	bookshelf
6	monitor	webcam	app store	speakers

ALL ABOUT ME

I'm usually ...
- shy.
- competitive.
- *(other)* ________

My best friends are ...
- kind.
- confident.
- funny.
- *(other)* ________

I want to visit ...
- Argentina.
- Egypt.
- Canada.
- *(other)* ________

I want to learn ...
- Chinese.
- Portuguese.
- Italian.
- *(other)* ________

I'm good at ...
- solving problems.
- thinking of new ideas.
- helping others.
- *(other)* ________

1 Complete the texts with the words in the box. There are three extra words you will not use.

a am anything at going to I'll made much often play playing solving the

Max: I love (1) ________ computer games. I have online friends all around the world, and we (2) ________ together. I'm really good at (3) ________ problems with computers. My friends always ask me for help when they have a problem. I hope (4) ________ be a computer programmer in the future.

Emmy: I like swimming and diving, and I'm good (5) ________ all kinds of sports. On weekends, I (6) ________ help my dad in (7) ________ garden because I love learning about plants and flowers. Last summer I spent some time planting trees in my local park.

Natasha: My favorite subject is history. I'll read (8) ________ about history, and I (9) ________ a history web page for my school project. I'm in the drama club at school, and I'm (10) ________ act in the school play next month.

2 Complete the table about the people in Exercise 1.

Life Skill	Max	Emmy	Natasha
School and learning	good at (1) *solving* problems	loves (5) ________ about plants and flowers	likes studying (8) ________ – her favorite subject
Getting a job	good with (2) c________s	interested (6) ________ plants, trees and flowers	good (9) ________ acting and interested (10) ________ history
Relaxing / Taking care of your health	loves playing (3) ________	good (7) ________ sports	loves (11) ________ history books
Using technology	goes (4) o________e to chat		designed a web page for school (12) ________

3 Choose the correct options from the box below to complete the conversation.

Li: What are your dreams for the future?
Jin: I'm not really sure. I'm interested (1) ____ math, so I (2) ____ be (3) ____ scientist. Right now (4) ____ astronomy, so maybe I (5) ____ study astronomy in college. I think there are (6) ____ careers I could choose.
Li: Do you want to live in this country, or (7) ____ else?
Jin: I'm sure I (8) ____ travel. My family (9) ____ to Puerto Rico last year, and we (10) ____ there again this winter. I'm (11) ____ learning languages and, in the future, I'm (12) ____ a lot of different countries. But I probably (13) ____ live in another country (14) ____ I like my home!

	a	b	c
1	a at	b with	c in
2	a will	b might	c am
3	a a	b the	c –
4	a I'll study	b I'm studying	c I studied
5	a will	b am going	c study
6	a a lot of	b much	c any
7	a everywhere	b somewhere	c nowhere
8	a will	b going to	c am
9	a go	b went	c were going
10	a go	b going	c are going
11	a not bad at	b bored with	c scared of
12	a going	b going to visit	c visiting
13	a might	b will	c won't
14	a because	b so	c and

4 Write sentences using the prompts.

1 Sally / do her homework / right now ?
____

2 We / have / a party / last weekend .
____

3 Tom / usually / 6:00 a.m. / get up ?
____

4 Our class / visit the zoo / yesterday .
____

5 I / probably / not win / the competition .
____

6 Victor and David / not watch / the soccer game / yesterday .
____

5 Correct the mistakes in bold in each sentence.

1 What **do you do** right now?
____

2 **I'm not knowing** the answer.
____

3 I **watched** TV when I heard a strange noise.
____

4 On Saturdays, **I'm** usually **playing** tennis.
____

5 I **was starting** school when I was five.
____

6 When **I'm buying** lunch, I saw my friend Eva.
____

Macmillan Education
4 Crinan Street
London N1 9XW
A division of Macmillan Publishers Limited

Companies and representatives throughout the world

ISBN 978-1-380-00771-1

Go Beyond First published 2015
First edition entitled *Beyond* published 2014

Designed by EMC Design Ltd.

Illustrated by Peter Cornwell pp. 18–19; Tom Croft pp. 12 (bottom), 24, 36, 44 (top); Venitia Dean (Advocate Art) p. 29; Cyrus Deboo p. 55; Mark Duffin pp. 8–9; Sally Elford pp. 6 (banner), 8 (banner), 18 (banner), 22, 23 (bottom), 28–29 (banner), 30 (banner), 40 (banner), 44 (bottom), 50–51 (banner), 52 (banner), 57, 62–63 (banner) 69-73 (banner); Guy Francis (Shannon Associates) pp. 17, 30, 39; Kory Heinzen (Shannon Associates) pp. 4–7; Bob Lea p. 12 (top); Chris Pavely pp. 21, 27, 43, 49, 52–53, 61.

Cover design by EMC Design Ltd.
Cover photograph by Getty Images/F1online/parasola parasola
Picture research by Tessa Hammond and Emily Taylor

The authors would like to thank all the team at Macmillan for everything they have done to make *Move Beyond* possible. We would like to thank Studio8 Ltd. and John Marshall Media, Inc. for their creative work on the videos, and the actors who bring the material to life. We would also like to thank John Marshall Media, Inc. for the production of the audio material. We would also like to thank all the teachers and other individuals who have contributed to the course whose names appear on this page.

The authors and publishers would like to express thanks to all those who contributed to the development and formation of *Move Beyond*. In particular, we would like to thank the following teachers, contacts, and reviewers: Cristina Moisén Antón, Argelia Solis Arriaga, Krzysztof Bartold, Paweł Bienert, Agnieszka Bojanowska, Samuel Gómez Borobia, Ma. Eugenia Fernandez Castro, Jolanta Chojnacka, Elsa Georgina Cruz, Dominika Dąbrowska, Barbara Dawidowska, Galina Dragunova, Monika Drygiel-Kobylińska, Mauricio Duran, Natalia Evdokimenko, Maria Teresa Velazquez Evers, Marciana Loma-Osorio Fontecha, Monika Fromiczew-Droździńska, Patricia Garcia, Axel Morales Garcia, Miguel Angel Rodriguez Garcia, Aleksandra Gilewska, Joanna Góra, Ewa Górka, Agata Helwich, Bethsabe Ruiz Herrera, Robert Jadachowski, Patricia Guzman Luis Juan, Anna Kacpura, Ruth Kanter, Regina Kaźmierczuk, Katarzyna Konisiewicz, Maria Koprowska, Bogusława Krajewska, Aldona Krasoń, Joanna Worobiec Kugaj, Joanna Kuligowska, Tadeusz Kur, Maria Kwiatkowska, Josefina Maitret, Claire Manners, Laura Elena Medina, Carmen García Méndez, Iwona Mikucka, Talhia Miranda, Claudia Rangel Miranda, Armando Nieto, Joanna Nowak, Anna Nowakowska, Ewa Nowicka, Anastasia Parshikova, Paloma Carrasco Peñalba, Ma. Del Carmen Fernandez Perez, Joanna Płatos, Maria Teresa Portillo, Juan Jose Gomez Ramirez, Aida Rivera, Gabriela Rubio, Gabriela Bourge Ruiz, Irina Sakharova, Małgorzata Sałaj, Patricia Avila Sanchez, Jessica Galvan Sanchez, Miguel Angel Santiago, Karol Sęk, Barbara Sibilska, Tatiana Sinyavina, Agnieszka Śliwowska, Vlada Songailene, Ángela Siles Suárez, Beata Świątkowska, Ewelina Szmyd-Patuła, Agnieszka Szymaniak, José Luis Vázquez, Irma Velazquez, Małgorzata Walczak, Dariusz Winiarek, Justyna Zdunek, Zofia Żdżarska, Dominika Zięba, Marzena Zieleniewska, Anna Zielińska-Miszczuk, Robert Zielonka.

The authors and publishers would like to thank the following for permission to reproduce their images:

Alamy/Steve Bloom Images p. 31(f), Alamy/Bubbles Photolibrary p. 34(tm inset), Alamy/Bruce Esbin-Anderson p. 43(cr), Alamy/Michael Flippo p. 40(e), Alamy/Foodfolio p. 40(d), Alamy/i love images p. 47, Alamy/Imagebroker p. 34(tl), Alamy/ImageSource p. 23, Alamy/Eric James p. 26(cr), Alamy/Frans Lemmens p. 31(d), Alamy/Jaak Nilson p. 17(cr), Alamy/OJO Images Ltd. p. 15(tr), Alamy/Alan Oliver p. 45(tr), Alamy/Photonic 3 p. 43(5), Alamy/Andres Rodriguez p. 10(tr), Alamy/Duncan Shaw p. 38(cr), Alamy/Paul Thompson Images p. 26(l), Alamy/John Trax p. 31(e), Alamy/Andrew Woodley p. 76, Alamy/World Travel Collection p. 30(b);
BrandX pp. 34(9, 11), 46(chicken wings, salads);
ComStock Images p. 46(cake, sushi);
Corbis p. 34(10), Corbis/Kai Chiang/Golden Pixels LLC p. 46(tl), Corbis/Odilon Dimier/PhotoAlto p. 56(cl), Corbis/Hero p. 46(tr), Corbis/Image Source p. 20(tr), Corbis/Ocean p. 48, Corbis/Piet/Cultura p. 34(tl inset), Corbis/Patrick Robert p. 33(tr), Corbis/Craig Tuttle/Design Pics p. 13(tr), Digital Vision p. 36(2,4,7);
Getty Images pp. 34(6), 51, Getty Images/Altrendo Images p. 15(cl), Getty Images/Asimetrica Juniper p. 42(omelette), Getty Images/Blend Images pp. 46(tm), 57, Getty Images/Mark Bowden p. 11, Getty Images/Dorling Kindersley p. 40(a), Getty Images/Jim Franco p. 20(br), Getty Images/Oliver Furrer p. 15(tl), Getty Images/Izabela Habur p. 25(b), Getty Images/Hill Street Studios p. 59(tl), Getty Images/kall9 p. 37, Getty Images/Janice Lin p. 15(b), Getty Images/Lonely Planet Images p. 30(c), Getty Images/Dwight Nadig pp. 30(a), 30–31, Getty Images/National Geographic RF p. 34(1), Getty Images/OJO Images pp. 40(c), 55(tr), Getty Images/Panoramic Images p. 13(tl), Getty Images/Barbara Peacock p. 56(tl), Getty Images/Radius Images p. 34(tm), Getty Images/SMC Images p. 35(tl), Getty Images/StockFood p. 45(cr), Getty Images/Jeremy Tan p. 43(2), Getty Images/Thinkstock p. 42(boy), Getty Images/David Tipling p. 35(br), Getty Images/Visuals Unlimited p. 35(tr);
Glow Images/Colin Anderson p. 55(cr), Glow Images/Mixa p. 43(1);
Image100 p. 34(8);
Image Source p. 46(sandwiches);
Passport NYC/Passport NYC 92Y 2012 pp. 40–41;
Photodisc pp. 34(3, 12), 43(3), Photodisc/Getty Images p. 46(pizza);
Plain Picture/Ableimages p. 38(tr), Plain Picture/fStop p. 22, Plain Picture/Image Source p. 10(cl), Plain Picture/Minden Pictures p. 34(tr), Plain Picture/Boro Monaco p. 43(4);
PowerStock p. 34(5);
Press Association/AP Images pp. 32, 33(tl);
Rex Features/Albanpix Ltd. p. 45(cl);
Thinkstock/Hemera p. 26(r), Thinkstock/iStock pp. 26(cl, c), 62, Thinkstock/moodboard p. 59(tr), Thinkstock/Photodisc p. 56(bl), Thinkstock/Photos.com p. 34;
Up The Resolution p. 46(cheese).

Commissioned photographs by Studio8 Ltd. pp. 25, 40(b).

Printed and bound in China

2021 2020 2019 2018 2017
10 9 8 7 6 5 4 3 2 1

MACMILLAN **ACADEMIC SKILLS**

Skillful
Listening&Speaking

Student's Book Pack

4

Authors: Lindsay Clandfield & Mark McKinnon
Series Consultant: Dorothy E. Zemach

Contents